D0063880

Books by Mary Ellen:

Mary Ellen's Best of Helpful Hints
Mary Ellen's Best of Helpful Kitchen Hints
Mary Ellen's Best of Helpful Hints Book II
Mary Ellen's Help Yourself Diet Plan
Mary Ellen's 1000 New Helpful Hints
Mary Ellen's How to Become a Healthier, Prettier You
How To Stop The One You Love From Drinking

by Mary Ellen Pinkham with her best buddy, Dale Ronda Burg
from New York City (who's always looking for work)

Illustrations by Jack Lindstrom

A Mary Ellen Book

The hints in this book are
intended to suggest possible
solutions only. The authors
and distributors cannot
guarantee absolute success.
To guard against damage, we
recommend you use care.

Mary Ellen Pinkham
Box 39221
Minneapolis, MN 55439

PRINTED IN THE UNITED STATES OF AMERICA

First Printing: March, 1992

ISBN 0-9631933-0-9

This book is dedicated to:
Tom, Dick and whoever Harry is.

Contents

Well, hello there!

Do you know any of these classic hints?

- To immobilize a bee, give it a shot of hair spray
- To keep cottage cheese fresh longer, store it upside down
- To make candles burn slower, store them in the refrigerator

They all appeared in my first book, *Mary Ellen's Best of Helpful Hints*. It came out in 1979 and was on the best-seller list for a year. I wrote three other best-selling collections after that, and now am pleased to issue this one — the first since 1984.

If you already own one of my books, or if you read my newspaper and magazine columns, then you know you can expect the pages that follow to be full of practical and fun-to-read ideas that save you time and maybe money, too!

In addition to writing, I've been busy on another project. My books are full of great home remedies, but you'll notice that I also recommend commercial products if they're the best solution for a particular job. In preparing my hint books and doing research, I was very aware that for some problems, there was no solution, or only an imperfect solution, be it a home remedy or commercial formula. For example: removing wine and coffee stains, blood stains and baby formula from fabric. A chemist helped me solve those problems, and others. And there is now a whole line of unique and — this is what makes me proud — truly effective Mary Ellen Home Care Products. (See information on back page if you have trouble finding them or want more information.)

Meanwhile, I've continued to collect helpful hints — ideas that make work easier, faster, cheaper and more fun. These are some of the best I've come across lately, and I hope you enjoy them.

Helpfully,

Mary Ellen

Fifty
Favorite
Hints

How Many Do You Know?

Which came first, the problem or the hint? This isn't nearly as tricky as the one about the chicken and the egg. The problem always comes first, and the hint is the solution. Obviously, hints aren't developed in laboratories. They come out of everyday experiences — mine and my readers. And since there are a lot of clever people in the world .. with a lot of the same problems... many people will come up with the same way to solve them. That's why the hints that follow are submitted to me time and time again. This doesn't mean that they aren't great ideas. On the contrary, they are great, because obviously they're so help-ful to so many people. That's why I consider them America's favorites. Sometimes I call them "starter" hints — because you shouldn't start a home without them! People who've been run-ning a house for a while usually enjoy looking over these hints to see how many they already know. I haven't yet run into any-one who knows them all.

Cleaning

- The best dustcloths: A pair of socks. Put one on each hand and use both at once.
- The cheapest window-cleaning solution: Windshield wiper fluid. Buy it by the gallon in the auto supply department.
- The best wiper for windows: Old newspapers. Cheap...and lint-free.
- Best home remedy for carpets: Blot up spill first, then satu-rate with club soda and/or Windex.
- Easiest way to clean inside a vase: Fill it with water, then drop in a denture tablet. After a brief soak, rinse it out.
- Best scum-proofing on shower doors: Clean it, then use lemon wax (or car wax). That repels soapy buildup.
- Greatest all-purpose deodorizers: Cat box filler. Coffee grounds. And crushed-up newspapers (Leave papers in a ther-mos bottle or sealed container for a couple of days; when you remove them, smell will be gone).

Recycling

- Best reuses for a fabric softener sheet: Keep drawers and luggage fresh. Wipe the lint screen of your dryer. Clean lint and pet hair off furniture. Eliminate static cling in skirts by rubbing on pantyhose.
- Smartest Christmas card makeovers: Cut out an element (character, flower, etc.) or a section of the card, punch a hole, attach string, use it as a Christmas tag.
- Smartest makeover for any card: Cut off front panel, use it as a postcard or note card.
- Most useful recycling of a plastic soda bottle: Make a disposable funnel from the top half. Cut a scoop from the bottom half.
- Or use the bottom half as a plant "greenhouse."
- Or turn the top into a yarn holder by slipping off the dark bottom "holder," cutting the bottom off the plastic bottle, slipping a ball of yard inside, feeding the strand through the neck, and replacing the dark bottom section.
- Cleverest substitutes for gift wrap: Kids' artwork; sheets from wallpaper sample books; comic pages from the newspaper; a small towel or receiving blanket (for a personal or baby shower).
- Thriftiest uses for ripped hose: Tie newspapers for recycling or blankets for storage; stuff children's toys; cover dryer and washer filters.
- Best use for an empty pump-top handsoap dispenser: Fill with liquid soap detergent.

Shopping

- Greatest shopping helper: A notebook to carry in your purse with clothing sizes and swatches, color samples and measurements for your decorating projects. Before you buy, you'll know whether the item is right.
- Most efficient grocery list: One that's written on the back of an envelope. Inside the envelope, keep your coupons.
- Handiest memory jogger (when buying a house, car, wedding gown): Take a Polaroid to review your possibilities at home and when you're not under pressure.
- Surest way to keep track of video rentals: Keep a list of possibilities in your purse, and cross them out as you rent — so you won't get the same one twice.

Kids

- Least painful removal of chewing gum from hair: Rub with some peanut butter or salad oil.
- Most effective way to keep kids out of the fridge: Put an insulated jug of cold drinks, with a spigot, on the counter. And give each child an individual, personalized plastic cup to avoid wasting paper all day long.

Kitchen

- Quickest way to reseal bag: Twist the top of the bag once, then turn the excess inside out and fold down over the rest of the bag.
- Easiest-cleaning shelf liners: Pieces of leftover linoleum. They're easy to cut for a custom fit, also durable and washable.

- Thriftiest use of leftover tea, coffee and soda: make ice cubes to put in cool drinks without watering them down.
- Simplest way to soften rock-hard brown sugar: Put a piece of cut apple or bread in the canister and wait a day or so. In a hurry? Grate it or microwave it.
- Neatest way to store recipes: Slip them into pages of a "magnetic" photo album. Pages are easy to remove for reference, splatters wipe off.
- Most popular way to keep from snacking as you cook: Sip water or chew gum.
- Best home remedy for keeping bugs out of flour or cereal: Put bay leaves or a stick of spearmint gum on the shelf.
- Easiest technique for removing fat from soup: Refrigerate the soup until the fat rises to the top and solidifies. Then lift it off with a spatula. (You can do this with canned soup too).

Planning

- Best insurance against being rear-ended by the garage door: Suspend a tennis ball from the garage ceiling so that it just touches the windshield when you've pulled all the way in.
- Most reassuring way to preserve your priceless family photographs: Store dearest negatives in your bank safe-deposit box.
- Best prevention against photos being lost at the developer: Put a name and address sticker on the film canister.
- Most foolproof way of keeping track of mail orders: Write the name and address of the company and if possible, what you've ordered, right on the check. In case you don't receive the item, you'll have the information for investigating the problem right at hand.
- Fastest way to make sure you've filled out a return address, sweepstakes entry, etc. correctly: Carry and use name and address stickers.
- Best precaution for sending get-well cards to a hospital: Put the patient's return address (rather than your own) on the envelope. If the patient has been discharged before the card arrives, it will be "returned" to his or her home.

Home Office

- Most organized system for storing warranties and appliance manuals: Keep warranties in a special file folder and appliance information in a folder or ring binder.
- Best letter-writing assist: Keep a separate envelope for everyone you want to write to, and as you find clippings, cartoons and other interesting items, drop them in. You don't have to write a lengthy note, yet the envelope will be full of things that are fun to read.
- Most fool-proof system for storing children's papers: At the beginning of each school year, buy a small accordion file folder (they expand and hold quite a bit), dropping in material as you go. If you ever get the time, you can sort them out. At least they're all together.

Laundry

- Best place to stash a waiting-to-be-ironed garment: In the freezer. It will be easier to iron...and it won't mildew.

Storage

- Most useful storage aids:
  - Plastic bags (particularly with zipper-type seals) can keep everything from jewelry to knitting supplies in good order.
  - Handyman's compartmentalized boxes for sorting nails and screws can also hold jewelry.
- Most space-saving way to store blankets: Tuck them into pillow shams and use as throw pillows.
- Least expensive way to make drawers smell nice:
  - Leave empty perfume bottles uncapped inside drawers.
  - Or insert a scented perfume sample ad from a magazine or department store mailing.
- Neatest way to stack bed linens: Fold pillowcases inside the sheet, and one sheet inside the other.
- Best preventative for mitten-cap-and-scarf clutter. Hang a multiple compartment shoe bag in the mud room or inside the closet door in the front hall — whichever's handiest.

As Good As New

I am the original pack rat. I hate to throw anything away because I'm sure that some day, it will come in handy. Often, that happens. For example: take miniskirts. I stored all of mine away in the early 70's when they went out of fashion, and sure enough, fifteen years later, they came back. Too bad my thighs of fifteen years before did not. I had no easy solutions for that problem...but I do have plenty of other fast and simple fix-it ideas to make something old look better or work better. These are some of my favorites.

Books are Musty

- To get rid of the odor, shake some dry starch onto the pages, then wipe away excess.

Bric A Brac is Broken

- If you have broken the knob of a sugar bowl or the hand from a figurine, use plumber's epoxy from a home center or plumbing supply shop to mold a new part. When it's dry, sand and attach with high-quality epoxy (that comes in two tubes). Paint with acrylic paint or colored nail polish. Give it a shiny glaze with clear nail polish or Future Floor Wax, or coat with an acrylic matte.

Can Opener is 'Frozen'

- If the cutting wheel is on your can opener is frozen, clean it with warm water and a bronze wire brush, then apply cooking oil liberally to the entire assemble. Wipe off the excess, rotate the wheel by hand...and you'll be ready to roll.

Carpet Pile is Flat

- Raise it with a steam iron. Build up a good quantity of steam, then hold the iron over the spot — without touching the carpet with the iron. Or put some ice cubes on the dent. When they've melted and dried, the pile will be raised.

Cedar has Lost its Scent

- To refresh an old cedar chest or closet, sand the inside of it gently with 00-grit sandpaper wrapped around a block of wood. You need remove only the thinnest layer. Then smooth any rough spots with 000- or 0000-grade steel wool. Always keep chest tightly closed.

Ceiling is Stained

- Those acoustical ceilings crumble if they're rubbed. Instead, just spray on a bleach and water mixture (but cover what's underneath so you don't get stains).

Door is Sticking

- If the door is sticking on a high spot, just tape a piece of rough sandpaper underneath. In a few days, normal usage will have done the sanding for you.

- If the door has swollen, there's too much moisture in it. An easy way to dry it out is to point your hair dryer, set on warm, at the places that stick. You may need to use a coat of sealant to prevent moisture from reoccuring.
- If you're about to install a thick carpet and think the door won't clear it, you don't have to shave the door down. You can install a rising butt hinge, which raises the door slightly as it opens. (Check the hardware and building supply stores.)

Drain is Clogged

- A sink that is clogged may just have grease caught in the trap. Direct a hair dryer set to hot under the trap until the grease has melted and flush the drain by running hot water for a few minutes. A wet/dry vacuum cleaner can be very effective to suction out a clogged drain.

Drawer is Stuck

- Remove the drawer and its contents or, if you can't, remove drawers near it. Aim a blow dryer set at medium at the drawer several inches from the wood. For a few minutes, move it back and forth along the drawer length. Once it's open, rub a bar of soap or candle on wood runners, or spray with furniture polish or non-stick vegetable spray. If runners are metal, use a light lubricant. If you have no blow dryer, leave a portable electric heater near dresser until the drawer can be pulled out, then proceed as above.

Foam Pillows and Pads are Limp

- Turn on the steam iron and hold the pads close enough to get a blast of steam. (My husband Tom owned an upholstery business and he's the one who passed this one on. He told me to use the same technique on my foam shoulder pads, too. Now both of us have shoulders to lean on!)

Glass is Nicked

- To repair small chips in your windshield or in mirrors, fill the indentation with clear nail polish.

Four of My Greatest Pickup Tricks

Now that I've got your attention, let me make it clear what kind of pickups I mean. I'm not talking about thrills...I'm talking about spills.

- If you're trying to pick up shards of broken glass, reach for a piece of bread! It's a better protector than a paper towel and you'd never reuse it, as you might reuse a sponge (so hidden pieces won't harm you).
- When you spill a lot of nails, pins or screws, retrieve them with a magnet wrapped in a paper towel. The magnet will attract the metal items through the paper — which you can then use to scoop them up.
- A disposable diaper is greatest thing in the world for mopping up a big spill.
- A neat way to get hair off the carpet or floor is to slip on a pair of rubber gloves. The hair draws toward it like a magnet but it won't stick to the gloves.

Hair Spray Can is Clogged

- I heard this one from a beauty parlor operator: She puts the stem in a bottle of rubbing alcohol, then sets it back in place, gives it a few squirts and it opens right up. She also saves the tip from empty cans to replace clogged tips from time to time.

Knives are Rusty

- This is a corker: Sprinkle cleanser on the blade and dampen a bottle cork. Scrub both sides of the knife with the flat end of the cork until the metal is clean. It's not that the cork has magic properties — just that its flat edge provides plenty of abrasion.

Marshmallows are Hard

- Place in an airtight container with a slice of bread for a few days.
- Put in a tightly sealed plastic bag and dip into very hot water.

- Or wrap them in a paper towel and microwave for 5-10 seconds on HIGH.

(This is also a good remedy for licorice, candy fruit and gumdrops.)

"Non-Stick" Pans are Sticky

- There may be an invisible film of food or grease residue on the pan. Remove it by rubbing the coating with a sponge dipped in vinegar or lemon juice, then wash thoroughly in hot, sudsy water.

Nuts are Stale

- Fry in a scant amount of oil.
- Marinate in lemon juice.
- If you keep them in the freezer, you won't have this problem.

Pans are Stuck Together

- If you've nested pans and can't pry them apart, place the two of them in the freezer for several hours, then bring a large pot of water to boil. Remove saucepans from the freezer and slowly set the bottom one into the boiling water. They'll come apart. (You can try a version of this when glasses are stuck together, filling the top with ice cubes and setting the bottom one in warm water — but I wouldn't advise this with delicate crystal.)

Paint is Nicked

You can try any of the following solutions:
- Matching shade nail polish works on many surfaces, even shoe heels! (You can buy it many colors these days, even black. Ignore the stares of the cosmetic saleswoman when you do; she's just envious you're young enough to wear punk nail polish. Artistic types can buy colorless nail polish and add food coloring mixed to desired shade.)
- Or store leftover paint in little nail polish bottles.
- Or buy small jars of paint meant to repair car nicks.

Plastic Item is Broken

- Broken items such as jewelry, children's toys and broken pot-
tery can often be repaired with with clear silicone sealer, available at auto supply stores. If any excess remains after gluing,
it can be shaped, molded or removed. Just dip your finger in
a solution of one part dishwasher detergent and 20 parts water,
then rub it off.
- Sometimes you can repair plastic items by heating the end of
a screwdriver or ice pick and touching it to the two broken
pieces just long enough to melt them; then clamp them back
together again.

Screw Slot is Worn

- Guess what! You don't have to replace the screw when the
screwdriver fails to get any leverage. Just get a hacksaw and
cut a new slot at right angles to the old one.

Shag Rug is Matted

- Occasionally give the rug a rake with a bamboo yard rake to
lift the pile.

Sponge is Slimy

- Soak it in a strong solution of vinegar and water for a day,
rinse several times in cold water. Leave dry — in sun, if possible. This works for loofahs, too.

Sweater has Yellowed

- If a white wool sweater yellows, give it a dye job — just as you
would your hair! After all, it's the sheep's hair.

Telephone Buttons are Sticking

- Use a small brush dipped in mineral spirits and wipe off excess.
Or try a very light spritz of vegetable spray or WD-40.

White Glue has Hardened

- Remove cap, then (for plastic bottle) place in boiling water
until glue softens or (for glass bottle) run hot tap water over
bottle for a minute or two, then place in simmering water.

- Place plastic bottle with top off in microwave at 15-second intervals (no longer, or you may have glue bubbling up, running over the side and onto the floor of your microwave).

Zipper Problems

- If it won't unzip easily, rub a zipper with a candle stub or lead pencil, or spray it with WD-40. Use the narrow extender tube so you don't get it on the fabric, or apply to a cotton swab and then swab it on the zipper.
- If it won't stay up, after it's zipped, spray it heavily with a hair spray containing lacquer. Let it dry and zipper will go up and down all day without slipping. Or sew a tiny button at the top and fasten a tiny elastic loop to the top of the zipper pull.

In a Pinch

- One tool that I've found handy to clamp small items is a hemostat, a surgical clamp, which you can get from the drugstore. But as a quick substitute, you can use a clip clothespin, adhesive tape, screw-type earring or a bit of florist's clay.

Life Extenders

- When the battery's failing: Rub it against an eraser.
- When the pen's running out of ink: Heat will give it a little more staying power. Dip it in boiling water.

Double Duty

What I mean by double duty is a thing that serves a purpose other than its obvious purpose. For example: a husband. While one obvious purpose of having a husband is to keep you from having to worry about a date for New Year's Eve, husbands are good for a lot of other things. Though frankly, if we're talking about a really outstanding entry in the double duty category, a Swiss army knife is what would come to mind.

Cut the Gadget Glut

You don't need a wall (or drawer) full of kitchen gadgets. Many of them can do two or more jobs. For example:

- Grapefruit knife also cuts corn off cob; also use it to section oranges.
- Melon ballers core apples, get cherries and olives out of the bottle.
- Pastry blenders mash eggs.
- Pancake turners stir soup. (Their flat bottom gets to the bottom of the pot more efficiently than a round spoon.)
- Pizza cutters cut brownies, separate slices of bacon, and cuts biscuits. (Pat batter square, and use the pizza cutter to make square biscuits — why not?)
- Percolators steam asparagus.
- Potato mashers break up ground meat.
- Potato peelers pit cherries and hull strawberries (use the tip), zest citrus rind, shave chocolate onto dessert or cheese onto omelets.
- Turkey basters water small plants or Christmas trees with no spills.
- Jumbo muffin tins make perfectly sized individual molded salads.
- Ice cream scoops measure muffin batter — and all the muffins will be just the same size.

Hair Dryer

- Set the icing on cakes (set on "warm medium"); perfect to help glue iced parts of gingerbread houses, too!
- Warm the bed for the kids.
- Thaw frozen pipes. (Hold it 6-8 inches away, set on medium, and wave it back and forth).
- Loosen photos so they can be peeled off pages of a "magnetic page" album.
- Loosen contact paper so it can be removed easily.
- Point it toward the gelatin mold from a distance of 6-8 inches until gelatin is loosened enough to unmold.

Skirt Hanger

- Will hold paint brushes to dry and keep them in shape.

Button

• Can solve a wobbly table leg problem. Just nail the button onto the bottom of the leg.

Toothpaste (Non-Gel)

• I've used white toothpaste as an instant spot remover on clothing while traveling. Dab it on, rub with a damp cloth and rub off.

Empty Shampoo Bottle

• Can be used to store oil to lubricate lawn mower, rototiller or other equipment with no fuss.

Toothbrush

• I know people who have so much trouble ending a relationship they can't even give up a toothbrush—even when the bristles look as if they've been steam rollered. Treat yourself to one that'll do some good for your teeth, and save the old one to: clean the grouting, polish the silver, rub away a stain on a garment.

Velcro

Who wouldn't love an invention that keeps your blouse from gapping and your waistband expandable? But that's not all this wonderful stuff can do. Here are some uses you may never have thought of:

• Use the pile side on the bottom of dining room chair legs to protect the floor from scratches.
• Attach it to the type of belt that just slips through the buckle, at the point where it's a comfortable fit. It never slips.
• If the hat's too big: put a strip of Velcro inside the brim. This is great for little kids who like to wear cowboy and fireman hats.
• If your vase is top-heavy — now there's a problem I can relate to — attach Velcro to the vase and to the stand.
• Put one strip of Velcro at the bottom of the remote control, and another strip on the arm of your favorite TV watching chair.

Glasses Cases
- Can hold folding scissors, small travel sewing kit.

Newspaper Plastic Bag
- Makes a fine elbow-length plastic glove.
- Carry in the diaper bag to chuck used diapers into.

Complimentary Shower Caps (from Hotels)
- These make fine bowl covers, shoe covers or covers for a camera lens on a rainy day.
- To catch the drips when watering a hanging houseplant, cover the bottom of the pot with a shower cap.

Hairpins
- Can train ivy. Push them in the ground to hold vine where you want it.

Skateboard
- Slip it under a heavy appliance or big potted plant and it'll skate right along.

Dish Drain Rack
- Use it to hold tacos while you're filling them.
- Us it as a pot lid holder in a cupboard.

Magnetic Knife Rack
- Inside medicine cabinet, will hold tweezers, scissors, etc.
- At work bench, can hold screw drivers, pliers, and other tools.

Vanilla Bean
- Two beans in a bottle of rum give it a delicious flavor
- Two beans in the sugar bowl (or in two cups of confectioners' sugar) make the sugar especially nice for coffee or for dipping strawberries .
- One or two beans in cake mix or in the milk for icing make it yummier.

- Two beans in the closet keep away the moths.
- Two beans under the carpet will perfume the house.

(How do you store vanilla beans? In a clean, tightly closed jar).

Oven Cleaner

- Removes oil-based paint from fabric: Spray the foam on work clothes stained with paint spots. Let stand for half an hour, then wash as usual. Safe for polyester and cotton, no matter if paint has dried on.
- Cleans a fiberglass tub! Spray the tub from bottom up with oven cleaner. Let stand half an hour or so, then wash down.
- Removes bathroom mildew: Spray tub, shower door, even shower curtain with oven spray, let stand five minutes, then clean up with a damp cloth.
- Cleans accumulated pitch and tar off power-saw blades! Spray and leave briefly, rinse.
- Warm encrusted non-aluminum baking dish in oven, then spray with oven cleaner. Cool, then wash with warm soapy water.

Plastic Milk Jug

- Make a 4 x 6 hole in it for kids to use as a crayon carrier with its own handle.

Mothballs

- Absorb moisture and prevent rust in a toolbox. Put in a dozen or so.
- Great pest repellents. Put into a sealed can with holes punched in it (so no harm will come to children or pets) and leave in areas where you have problems with spiders, raccoons, etc.

Electric Blanket

- Lay it over a large piece of flooring that won't uncurl. The heat may do the trick.

Bleach

- I clean my veggies and fruit with liquid bleach and cold water. Just add 1/4 cup bleach to a sinkful of cold water. Let produce soak for 15 minutes and then rinse thouroughly.

Bag of Frozen Vegetables

• Make a pliable, instant ice-pack.

ID Card

• Take an expired credit card, trim off your name and leave enough surface to punch a hole, and you've got yourself a weatherproof ID tag for tools and other gear.
• Keep one in the kitchen to scrape dough off counter or board.

Carpet Piece

• The wife of a carpeting installer told me that when using any cleaning solution on carpeting of any type, use another piece of carpeting as the scrubber. I've found this to be an excellent aid in removing spots and stains, old and new.
• Put a piece in the botton of your tote bag to keep the bag's shape.
• Or use a flat piece inside your kids boots as a warm inter-lining.
• Slide under heavy objects (pile side down) and they'll slip along the floor.

Liquid Soap

• The kind formulated to remove grease from dishes makes an excellent instant stain remover on clothing.
• Liquid Dial Soap is fantastic for cleaning chopping blocks. It contains a germ killer. Use it to clean your eyeglases too. Nothing works better.

Ammonia

I like the cooking part of being in the kitchen, it's the cleaning up part I hate. How about those dirty pots and pans? Clean them the Mary Ellen way and you'll get out of the kitchen sooner.
• Drop those impossible to clean pans (do not use on aluminum) in a heavy duty trash bag. Pour in about 1 cup of ammonia. Tie the bag shut and set it outdoors or in the garage overnight. Ammonia is powerful so be sure to turn your head away from the fumes while opening the bag. Now, rinse the pans off with soap and water and the greasy grime will slide off. When the weather is nice, I do the rinsing with my garden hose right on the driveway.

WD-40

- Spray it on the car, wipe off tar.
- If you give the car lock a spritz of WD-40, in cold weather it's less likely to freeze.
- Removes stickers and adhesives from glass.
- Loosens stuck light bulbs.
- Removes gum from clothing.
- Helps remove a tight ring from finger.
- Spray on boots before tracking through mud and the mud won't stick.
- When buttons on a phone or calculator stick, spray on a bit of WD-40.

Borax

- To deodorize the carpet, sprinkle on 20 Mule Team Borax, leave it for an hour, then vacuum.
- If you want your brushes to be clean, fresh and smelling sweet, bathe them in a basin of warm water, 1 tablespoon soap or detergent, and half a cup of Borax.
- If you act quickly, you may be able to remove a wine stain from the carpet. Add 1 part Borax to three parts water, and sponge some of the mixture onto the stain. Leave for half an hour, shampoo the area. After it's dried, vacuum it up.

Silicone Spray

- Tight fitting cowboy boots will go on easier if you spray the insides with silicone spray. They'll slip right on and off. It also helps control foot odor.

Spray Mount

- A throw rug will stay in place if you give it two or three squirts of Spray Mount (available at office supply stores).

Hands On

Applique

Bar Service: A sliver of soap is a great "pencil" when you're drawing a design for applique (or embroidery). If you want to get fancy, you can actually carve a "crayon" with a point from the sliver. A bit of water dabbed on with a sponge or the corner of a piece of clean cloth is your eraser. Washing the item will remove the soap when you're finished with your work.

Shirt Order: To applique a sweatshirt, trace the pattern onto fusible interfacing, iron the interfacing to the applique fabric and cut out the shape. Backing will keep the material from wrinkling and pulling up, and it can be pinned and sewn on nice and flat with a large, zigzag stitch.

Design Inspiration: Coloring books are a good source of traceable applique patterns. Cookie cutters in animal and other shapes also make interesting patterns — with a wide variety of options to choose from.

Fasten-ating: Tape appliques instead of pinning them and there won't be any marks. Pink tape from the beauty salon will hold the material in place yet peel off easily.

Beading

Separation Anxiety: Use an egg carton or ice cube tray to keep tiny beads and sequins separated by color and type. Or save your film canisters for this purpose. Glue a bunch of canisters to a small piece of board and have a portable setup.

Crochet

Clip Service: That last crochet stitch will stay in place when you put your work away if you clip a clothespin on it.

Shapely Suggestion: Shape a starched or glued crocheted basket by setting it to dry on top of an inverted, foil-covered bowl of the proper size.

Square Deal: When crocheting together afghan squares, use a chain stitch between each double crochet to prevent tightness.

Cross-Stitch

Wrinkle protection: If you spray-starch your cross-stitch picture before you iron it, it will be less likely to wrinkle in the frame.

Embroidery (see also Needlepoint)

You're Stranded: To divide a six-strand embroidery floss the easy way, cut the length that you want and then moisten it with a damp sponge. The strands will come apart easily and will dry almost immediately.

Keeping Tabs: The plastic price tabs from bread bags can hold embroidery thread. Wind thread from top to bottom and make a tiny horizontal slit in the tab to secure the ends.

Two in One: Here's a combination place holder and needle-holder. Glue a magnetic strip to a spring clothespin. Use the clothespin to keep your instruction book open, and park the needle on the magnet when you're changing floss.

Knitting

Small Change: If you drop a stitch, pick it up with a smaller size needle. You'll end up with a small, even stitch instead of a big, loose one.

Needle Holder: To make a container your knitting needles won't slip out of, use a shoe box. Just poke needles through the cardboard at one end, matching needle numbers in pairs. Or store needles in an empty paper-towel tube, taping one end to keep them from falling out.

On Your Mark: When working a long piece of knitting, put markers at regular intervals along seam edges. When sewing up the pieces, match the markers.

Double Time: Always knit sleeves, pockets and other items at the same time, using circular needles to hold both sets if necessary. Then they'll be exactly the same length. Be sure to complete the same row on both needles before you put your work aside.

Pick Lock: Use brightly colored plastic toothpicks to hold edges of a knitted garment together while sewing. They're easy to see and slip in and out of stitches.

Stretch it Out: If you don't have enough yarn to finish a row, unravel a couple of rows. This stretches the yarn for extra inches.

Good Stuff: Leftover bits and pieces of yarn? If you don't want to use them in a patchwork rug, use them to pack stuffed toys for children.

Inch It Along: Before starting any knitting project, take one needle and, using a dot of nail polish, mark off six inches at 1-inch intervals. Let polish dry thoroughly. Now you won't have to search for a tape measure any more. You'll have one right at hand.

Back in Shape: If you want to reshape circular knitting needles, place them briefly in water that's been heated to simmer. Repeat process if necessary and press needles between thumb and finger to uncurl them. Steel ones must be stretched out straight, uncurled and reshaped, then put under a heavy weight for a week or so.

Following Instructions:

- Use a music stand to hold instructions, pictures, yarn or floss while working on needlecraft or knitting projects.
- Rewrite knitting instructions on 3x5 cards, different colors to mark repeat rows.

Packed Away: Quantities of yarn (and material, too) can be kept dust-free in garbage cans lined with a plastic garbage bag. And a clear tennis ball carton holds a skein of yarn perfectly. Cardboard tubes can also hold leftover lengths of yarn (fabric, too). The label with information about the yarn (or fabric), such as gauge and care instructions, can be stored inside the tube.

Stringing Along: An oatmeal box is a fine yarn skein holder. It keeps the yarn clean, and you can punch a hole in the top of the box to draw the yarn through a bit at a time.

Miscellaneous

Bits and Pieces: If using Styrofoam bits, dip your hand in water before picking up a handful. There won't be any static.

Made for Measure: Attach one end of the tape measure to an old spool with a hot glue gun or a stapler. You can wind it up for storage, slip it onto a spool holder in your sewing case, I've found it's harder to misplace.

Slice and Easy: The easiest way to cut foam rubber is with an electric carving knife.

One Good Turn: Put small ceramic or other painting projects on a lazy susan or old turntable. They can be turned easily.

Mark This: Always include a label of your yarn when you give someone a knitted or crocheted present and when you donate a handmade item to a bazaar. The labels should supply not only cleaning instructions but also fiber content in case someone has an allergy.

Painting

Brush Up: Clean brushes by soaking for 15-20 minutes in Lestoil, rinse and dry. And use Lestoil to remove paint from clothes and hands.

Canvas Cleaner: Reclaim a painted canvas by spraying it with oven cleaner. Set it in the sun for several hours, rinse with garden hose and repeat until canvas is clean and ready to repaint.

Patterns

Getting Around: To make a circular pattern, tie a piece of string to a tack. Attach the other end to a pencil stub or chalk piece. Place the tack in the center of whatever you wish to mark, wind the string around the the pencil until you have the correct radius. Then draw your circle.

Tray Bien: Don't toss out styrofoam meat trays. Wash them thoroughly and save for craft projects. They're sturdy enough to use as cutouts for stencils or patterns for appliques.

Big Time: Enlarge a craft pattern by taking it to a copy shop, where they can do an enlargement automatically, quickly and for pennies. And next time you're using Contac paper, save the liner with the l" grid and use it to enlarge patterns for future craft projects such as appliqued patterns.

Following the Guidelines: Freezer wrap paper is great for tracing craft patterns. You can see through it and write on it — and it's durable enough to reuse.

Needlepoint

Present under Glass: Framing your needlepoint under glass will keep it clean and dust-free, but do take care. The glass shouldn't rest directly on your work. Be sure to lay a thick cardboard framing mat over it before you put it under the glass.

What a Sketch: When you're tracing a design placed underneath a needlepoint canvas or drawing freehand on it, you'll find it's easier if you pull the pencil toward you instead of trying to push it away from you.

Stitcher's Block: Afraid the colors will run when you block your needlepoint? Shake a good coating of salt on your work before you wet it, and use cold water. Block to correct size and shape, secure with rust-proof pushpins, then allow to air dry.

Dust Cover: Vacuum your needlepoint pictures every once in a while and they'll stay fresher looking.

Quilting

Marking Time: Use slivers of soap, rather than chalk, to mark quilting. The needle slides right through the marks.

Patching Things Up: When using a very large piece of fabric for quilting, first preshrink it, then press iron-on interfacing on the back. Shapes and cutting lines can be drawn on the interfacing, and the added body will make quilting faster and the quilt easier to handle.

Sewing

It's a Snap: If snaps have broken off a robe or other garment, sew a Velcro dot over the top snap (or in the place where the snap used to be), and remove and replace the bottom snap with another Velcro dot.

Punch In: Use a hole punch to make holes in a pattern so you don't have to keep pinning through it. And use a small paper punch to mark holes at notch point, then use a pen to mark the spot.

Design Plan: One way to get patterns at very low cost is to find clothing bargains at garage sales, then take the items apart with a seam ripper. Trace them on butcher or freezer paper.

Cut It Short: To shorten slacks without a partner to pin them, stand sideways in front of the mirror. Hitch up pant leg at the thigh until the pants bottom is at the level you desire. Pin tuck formed at thigh, measure material taken up by tuck, and take this amount off the pants bottom.

Get It Together: Purchase a garment bag used for sweater storage to store your fabric and sewing notions. Hung in the closet and out of the way it keeps them organized, dust-free and highly visible.

On The Button: A drop of clear nail polish keeps machine-sewn buttons in place. Or use a carefully placed drop of super-glue. It fuses threads, and buttons stay on permanently.

It's a Draw: To replace drawstring in sweats, sew a piece of ribbon to each end of a length of elastic, use a safety pin to pull one end through.

Pattern Cutting Trick: Use pinking shears to cut the pattern for the front, regular shears to cut the pattern for the back. You'll never get the two confused.

Difficulty Reading a Pattern: If you have the pattern copied at the copy store it may come up sharper.

Making a Pattern Bigger: To enlarge a pattern by hand, using the grid on a cutting board (marked into one-inch squares) may help. Easier still, take it to a copy shop where they can do the enlargement automatically.

Easiest Ways

- The easiest way to get tomato sauce off plastic storage containers: Just leave them in the sun! The bleach clean.

- The easiest way to keep appliances clean: Apply some good car wax to the front of the dishwasher, stove and refrigerator. The hard surface will resist dirt; and it will be easy to wipe clean.

- The easiest way to remind yourself that an article of clothing needs spot cleaning: Tie a loose knot in any piece of clothing with stains that need special attention before laundering.

Homemade

Out of my "recipe" files, I've selected the following. Some, like the lasagna and pie, are personal favorites because they're quick, easy and delicious. Others, like the Friendship recipes, are those that readers of my column have asked me to track down. And still others aren't recipes for eating at all — but formulas for homemade solutions that do a wonderful job.

Friendship Baked Goods

The following recipes work like a kitchen chain letter and are known by a variety of names, among them Friendship Cake, Amish Cake, Herman Cake, Moonshine Cake, and Louisiana Love Cup. They begin with a "starter" or "herman" that you prepare over several weeks; when it's done, you give a part of it to a friend. The recipes, like friendship, require time and effort...and the results are worth it. (But I've never figured out who "herman" is or was.)

Friendship Bread

Making the Starter

Day 1: Soften 1 package active dry yeast with 1/4 cup warm water for 10 minutes. Stir, using a wooden spoon. In a non-metal bowl, combine 1 cup each flour and sugar. Mix. Slowly add 1 cup warm (110°) milk and softened yeast. Cover loosely and leave at room temperature until bubbly. Refrigerate.

Day 2,3, and 4: Stir until smooth with wooden spoon.

Day 5: Blend 1 cup flour and 1 cup sugar. Add 1 cup milk. Stir into starter. Return to refrigerator.

Day 6,7,8,9: Stir once a day.

Day 10: Repeat day 5.

Using the Starter
- You may use some for baking, give some away, and/or store some in freezer. (Takes three hours to thaw, then behaves as if fresh.)
- To keep it going, store remainder in fridge and feed, following the 10 day cycle. If you're getting too much, cut the "food" in half on one feeding, but don't let it drop below 1 cup because to rejuvenate to usable amounts takes several days. To use, take what you need out of fridge, allow to come to room temperature (and wait until it's very bubbly).

Making the Bread
- Mix 2 cups flour, 1 cup sugar, 1-1/4 teaspoons baking powder, 1/2 teaspoon baking soda, 1/2 teaspoon salt, 1/2 teaspoon cinnamon.
- Then add 2 cups starter, 2/3 cup vegetable oil, 3 lightly beaten eggs, 1/2 teaspoon vanilla and mix well.
- Add 1 to 2 cups of optional ingredients such as nuts, dates or other dried fruit, chocolate chips, apples or applesauce, bananas, zucchini or carrots.
- Bake in 2 well-greased 9x5 loaf pans at 350° about 45-55 minutes.

Friendship Cake

Step 1 -Making the Starter Liquid (6 weeks)
- Mix 1 cup canned pineapple chunks, 1 cup sugar and 2 teaspoons brandy in one gallon jar with lid. Cover and leave at room temperature , stirring daily.
- Day 14: Add 1 cup maraschino cherries with liquid, 1 cup sugar and 2 tablespoons brandy. Cover and stir daily.
- Day 28: Add 1 cup canned peaches with syrup, 1 cup sugar, 2 tablespoons brandy. Cover and stir daily. Wait two more weeks and it is ready to use. Drain fruit, reserving the liquid. (Use the fruit for serving over pudding or ice cream, or topped with whipped dream.)

Step 2 - Making the Starter Fruit (30 days)
- Combine 1-1/2 cups starter liquid (as prepared above), 2-1/2 cups sugar, and a 28-oz. can of sliced peaches with syrup. Cover loosely and store at room temperature, stirring daily for 10 days.
- Day 10: Add 2-1/2 cups sugar and a 16-oz can of crushed pineapple. Stir daily.
- Day 20: Add 2-1/2 cups sugar, a 16-oz can fruit cocktail with syrup, and a 10-oz jar of maraschino cherries with liquid. Stir daily.
- Day 30: Drain fruit, reserving the liquid, and divide it into 4 equal parts. Each part will make one cake. Divide liquid into 1-1/2 cup portions and give to friends to make a new batch of fruit. (They should begin at Step 2). Save one portion for yourself, but don't refrigerate (since that stops fermentation action). Use fruit in the recipe below.

Step 3: Baking the Cake
- Mix and beat until smooth 1 box yellow cake mix, 1 small box of instant vanilla pudding, 1/2 cup vegetable oil and 4 eggs. Stir in 1 cup chopped nuts and 1 portion of the fruit mixture. Bake at 350 in a greased and floured 9 x 13 or bundt pan for 45-55 minutes or two 8x8 pans for 35-40 minutes. Top with whipped cream or a cream cheese frosting (Blend 1 stick butter, 1 8 oz. package cream cheese, 1 pound confectioner's sugar, 1 teaspoon vanilla).

ROAST BEEF

Gracie Allen's Classic Recipe for Perfect Roast Beef.

1 large roast of beef
1 small roast of beef

Take the two roasts and put them in the oven. When the little one burns, the big one is done.

Lazy Lasagna

I love this recipe because 1) it couldn't be easier to make and 2) who doesn't like lasagna? The secret is starting with dry noodles. When I first made it up, there was no such thing as a "no-cook" lasagna noodle on the market. Now there is, but in fact, any lasagna noodle is fine for this recipe.

You need: aluminum foil and a 9" x 13" dish.

1   16-oz. box of lasagna noodles
2   15-oz jars any spaghetti sauce
1   16- oz. container ricotta cheese
1   8-oz package sliced mozzarella
     Grated parmesan cheese

Optional: 1 lb. ground beef or turkey. (Brown this in a skillet and add it to the sauce before you begin.)

     Garlic (I just pour in a lot)
     Fennel (A spice that gives the illusion of sausage without the
          fat and calories)

Assembly:

Pour about 1/2 cup sauce in the dish. Cover with uncooked noodles laid side by side. Evenly distribute half the riccota, half the mozzarella, and a third of the sauce over the noodles. Repeat this step. Top with a third layer of noodles and remaining sauce. Sprinkle with parmesan. Cover with foil. Bake at 350° for one hour, covered. Remove from oven and leave for 20 minutes covered. Then uncover and eat.

Hollywood Pie: My favorite fast dessert

• Some people think I call this Hollywood Pie since it's sweet and rich. Nope. I gave it this name after I spent some time on a movie set: it, too, requires a lot of waiting around but only five minutes of work. Chill one 14-oz can sweetened condensed milk for two hours. Add 2 tablespoons of lemon juice and beat with electric mixer on high speed for five minutes or until it becomes white and thick (like pudding). Spoon into a store-bought 9-inch graham cracker crust and chill several hours. Top with fresh or frozen fruit and whipped cream.

Fourth of July Cake: Very showy, very easy

- Make a sheet cake of plain vanilla and decorate it like a flag. Use whipped cream alternated with sliced strawberries for stripes, and pipe whipped cream stars on a bed of blueberries.

Quick and Easy White Sauce

- Blend together 1 cup flour and 1 cup butter. Spread evenly in an ice cube tray and refrigerate. Cut into 16 cubes, place in a plastic bag and store in the freezer. When ready to use, add 1 cube to 1 cup milk and heat slowly, stirring constantly.

Ice Cream Muffins

- Blend a softened pint of vanilla ice cream with two cups of biscuit mix just until moistened, divide batter into a dozen greased muffin cups and bake at 350° for 20 minutes. Now, that's easy!

Tomato Jam

- Boil three cups of peeled chopped ripe tomatoes with two cups of sugar for 10 minutes. Add one thinly-sliced lemon and one 3-oz. box of lemon gelatin and boil another 10 minutes. Put in clean hot jars and seal.
- Or add 4 cups sugar to 5 cups chopped or ground green tomatoes. Boil hard for 7 minutes, then add two 3-oz. packages of raspberry or strawberry gelatin and pour in clean, sterilized jars and seal.

Flower Preservatives (Real and Artificial Flowers)
Washing Soda Solution (for real flowers)

- Either leave the stem on the flower or remove it just below the base of the calyx, which is the green, leafy part of the flower. Place flower in box containing mixture of 1 part Borax and two parts corn meal. Gently, without crushing the petals, cover the flower with more of the mixture. (With many-petaled flowers, such as carnations and roses, sprinkle the mixture directly into the flower blossom before placing flowers in the box). Leave no air space around the flower and don't let flowers touch one another.

- Seal box with tape and store at room temperature in a dry place for 7-10 days. Gently pour off enough mixture until you can grasp flower with two fingers, then pour off rest. Clean off any clinging mixture with a soft artist's brush. (If petals are broken off, they may be reglued.). Strain mixture to remove debris, then store in cool dry place for future reuse. If mixture becomes moist, bake it in a low oven — about 200 degrees — for an hour.

- (Please note: This may not work on cut flowers that have been put in a water to which preservative has been added by a florist or by you.)

Glycerine Solution (for real flowers)

- Make up one cup glycerine dissolved in a quart of hot water, with a teaspoon of chlorine bleach to absorb bacteria. Submerge the plants or just place stems in the mixture. The mixture has been absorbed when you see drops of moisture form around the edges of the leaves. Remove the flowers and hang them upside down — a pants hanger is helpful. When dry, they will be tough and somewhat pliable.

Foliage Preserver (for autumn leaves)

- Place stems in one part glycerine (buy it at the drug store) and two parts water, and let them drink it up. Foliage will keep for years.

Preservative Dip (for artificial flowers; keeps them from fading)

• Blend one cup each of turpentine and fruitwood stain, then stir in two tablespoons of gold powder (from the craft shop) until you have a soupy paste. Cut top off clean, empty juice carton, pour mixture in, and insert flowers upside down, moving them gently through the mixture until coated. Hang plants upside down — for example, by using a clothespin to fasten them to an indoor clothesline — until dry. Coat with colorless enamel spray (following directions on can).

Home Repair

Spackle

Any of the following solutions can be used instead of spackle and applied with your fingers instead of a putty knife. Of course this won't be as strong as the real thing, but just avoid these spots when you're going to make a nail hole.

- Mix white glue and baking soda.
- Or mix talcum powder with boiled linseed oil until it gets to the right consistency.
- Toothpaste also does the job.
- Or get hold of some of the baby's Play-Doh©.

Burn Coverup

- Mix equal amounts — as little as an ounce— of water, isopropyl alcohol (that's rubbing alcohol) and glycerin. You can get the last two from the drug store. Apply to burned area, let set until burned color has disappeared. Rinse with water and dry. If burned part hasn't been completely removed, use a mild abrasive or fine steel wool. If there's a depression in the wood, use a color touchup.

Wallpaper Paste

- One cup of Argo starch, moistened with enough water to make a paste. Add boiling water and it will turn glossy. Add just enough boiling water to make into a thin paste that can be applied with a brush, then add two to three heaping teaspoons of sugar to the mixture.

Child's Play

Finger Paints

- Soak 1 envelope unflavored gelatin in 1/4 cup water. Combine 1/2 cup cornstarch and 3 tablespoons sugar, then gradually add 2 cups water. Cook slowly over low heat, stirring constantly about 5 minutes. Remove from heat and add gelatin mixture. Divide into containers and add a drop or two of liquid dish detergent. Then stir in food coloring.

Play Clay

- Mix 2 cups flour and 1 cup salt, then stir in 1/2 c
  1 teaspoon vinegar. Knead until soft, divide into p
  knead food coloring into each. (Store in refrige
  indefinitely.)

Cleaners

Bathroom

- Combine a gallon of warm water with 1/2 cup washing soda
  or Borax, 1/2 cup white vinegar and 1/2 cup ammonia. This
  will remove soap scum and is an excellent tile and fixture
  cleaner. Washing soda is available in hardware stores.
- For extensive stains on colored tile make a paste with 3 parts
  Borax with 1 part 3% hydrogen peroxide, on white tile, make
  a paste of Borax with bleach. Scrub with a brush and rinse
  thoroughly.

Pine

- This solution saves you about 40% off the supermarket price,
  using 1 cup mineral oil, 1 tablespoon pine oil, 1/4 cup soap
  flakes, 1 cup warm water: In a glass bowl, mix the mineral oil,
  pine oil. Stir in soap flakes and water. Store in a clean, quart
  jar. To use, pour a tablespoonful onto a cloth. Polish, then
  buff with clean cloth.

Lemon-Scented Spray

- This one is incredibly easy to make. Just combine a cup of
  mineral oil and a teaspoon of lemon oil. Then pour them
  into a clean, spray bottle. Be sure to shake the mixture before
  using . And don't forget to use a clean cloth to buff.

Upholstery Cleaner

- Combine half a cup of mild detergent and 2 cups of boiling
  water. It will cool down to form a jelly. Then beat it with an
  egg beater until it's foamy. Apply it like a paste over the upholstery — and when it's dry, vacuum it off.

Never mix any chlorine product (such as bleach, mildew remover, tile cleaner, powdered cleansers) with any of the following:

- Automatic dishwasher detergent. It creates an acid that will eat away at flatware and pots.
- Ammonia. It creates an acid that will eat away at your appliances or any other metal surface.
- Acids (such as toilet bowl cleaners). Very hazardous gases may result.
- Baking Soda. Hazardous gases may result.

Read labels carefully. Old products are reformulated and new products may list new cautions.

Cloths

Polishing

- Store-bought polishing cloths costs five times what these do. Cut a yard of flannel, cotton or terry cloth into six-inch squares. Moisten them with water, put them in a large plastic container and saturate with a mixture of 1/4 cup water and 1 cup mineral oil and 1 teaspoon lemon oil (from craft store). Shake well, immediately pour over cloths. Wipe furniture; buff with clean cloth. Reuse until soiled and then discard — or wash and reuse.

Dusting

- Put a couple of teaspoons of turpentine in a quart of hot, sudsy water. Get yourself some clean, lint-free cloths, stick them in the jar, cover and let them soak overnight. Wring and let dry. You'll be surprised at how effectively these attract dust.

- An alternative: mix two cups hot water with a quarter cup of lemon oil, saturate cloth and let hang dry. Not for wood.

Cleaning Solutions

Chandelier Cleaner
- Mix one part isopropyl alcohol and three parts distilled water.

Walls
- This costs pennies — a comparable commercial product is 20 times the price. Combine 1/2 cup Borax, 2 tablespoons soap flakes, 1 tablespoon ammonia, one gallon warm water. Store in plastic jug. Use full strength in spray bottle or add two cups to a pail of warm water.

Windows
- For a home-made cleaner, this does a terrific job. Combine 1 cup white vinegar and 1 cup ammonia; add 1 tablespoon mild detergent. Pour into a one-gallon jug and fill with water. Pour into a spray bottle to use, let set for 1/2 minute. Then wipe off with paper towels or newspaper.
- Or mix 1/2 cup ammonia, 1/2 cup of white distilled vinegar and two tablespoons of cornstarch to a bucket of warm water for another fine window-washing solution.

Dishwasher Anti-Spotter
- I love to add this to my dishwasher — especially when I'm doing a load of crystal. Combine 1 cup Borax and 1/2 cup baking soda, and add a teaspoon of the mixture to your dishwasher detergent with each load.

Mirrors
- Combine two tablespoons of ammonia to 1 quart of water for squeaky clean mirrors.

All-Purpose Cleaner

- Depending on the job, use this either full-strength or diluted. Pour 1/2 cup ammonia and 1 cup washing soda into a clean plastic gallon jug. Add two cups warm water, cover and shake. Then add twelve more cups of water. Label the jug so everyone knows it's cleaner, please. Use 1/2 cup to a bucket of water for large jobs, full strength in a small bottle for appliances and tile.

Laundry

Prewash Spray

- This laundry pretreatment spray that will cost you only about a quarter per gallon calls for ammonia, white vinegar, baking soda, granulated non-chlorine laundry detergent. Mix 1/2 cup ammonia, 1/2 cup white vinegar, 1/4 cup baking soda, 2 tablespoons granulated detergent and two quarts of water in a gallon jug and shake well. Pour into a spray bottle, spritz stain, let it set for a minute or two and then launder.

Spray Starch

- Here's my two cents worth! — spray starch for only two cents. Just add four teaspoons cornstarch to two cups of water, mix and put into a spray bottle. Spray on clothing, then iron. And if you want a nice scent — add a bit of fragrance to the mixture. About 1/2 teaspoon of cologne will do the job.

Personal

Bubble Bath

- Combine two cups of vegetable oil, three tablespoons of liquid shampoo and a thimbleful of your favorite perfume. Beat the mixture in a blender at high speed for several seconds, then add to the tub and enjoy.

- Mix 3/4 cup Joy, 1 gallon water, and a tablespoon of glycerine.
- Or four cups powdered soap, 4-6 drops glycerine and (for the kids), food coloring.
- Or 4 T cornstarch, 15 T cream of tartar, 18 T of baking soda. Three tablespoons of this mixture will give you a tub full of bubbles.

Hand Lotion
- Add 1-1/2 quarts of water to 1/2 oz. of gum traganth, and let stand for 24 hours. Then add 1 oz. tincture of benzoin (plain) and 4 oz. each of cologne and glycerine. Stir well, and add water if it's too thick. You can get all ingredients from your pharmacist, and this is terrific for chapped hands.

Jewelry Cleaners

For Gold
- Combine one-half cup of clear household ammonia and one cup of warm water. Let chains or rings sit in the solution for ten to fifteen minutes. Scrub jewelry with soft brush and rinse under warm water — with the sink drain closed.

For Diamonds, Rubies and Sapphires
- Mix in a bowl one cup of water, one-quarter cup of ammonia and a tablespoon of dishwashing detergent. Scrub lightly with an old toothbrush. Ammonia won't hurt gold or silver settings.
- Do not use this formula for cleaning soft, porous stones such as opals, pearls, turquoise and coral.

For Silver
- For quick clean-ups when no silver polish is available, dab on some toothpaste and rub with a damp cloth. Buff with a clean cloth.

Liqueurs, Homemade

I no longer drink — I've had enough! But I know many of you enjoy moderate amounts of liqueurs as dessert, and you should enjoy these budget-wise recipes.

Kahlua

4 cups sugar
2 cups water
6 tablespoons freeze-dried coffee or 3 tablespoons instant
3 cups vodka or light rum
1-2" vanilla bean

Boil the sugar and one and one half cups water and the vanilla bean broken in several places for 30 minutes. Dissolve the freeze-dried or instant coffee in one-half cup of boiling water. Shake together the sugar syrup and the coffee solution. Add alcohol and glycerine. Let it stand two weeks in a covered jar. Remove the bean. Store the liquid in a tightly covered glass container. Makes 2-l/2 pints.

Amaretto

7 cups sugar
4 quarts water
l cup dark Karo syrup
l teaspoon freeze-dried coffee
4 oz. almond extract
2 oz. vanilla extract
l fifth grain alcohol
(optional) caramel coloring.

Boil sugar, water and syrup for 50 minutes. Add coffee and cool to room temperature. Combine with remaining ingredients. Enjoy.

Orange Liqueur

3 whole sweet oranges, cut into wedges
l/2 lemon
2 whole cloves
3 cups vodka
l cup sugar
l/2 cup water

Place the oranges, lemon, cloves and vodka in a jar. Make sure vodka covers the fruit. Steep ten days, turning and shaking jar gently every few days. Strain and filter. Boil the water and sugar together until sugar dissolves. Set aside and cool. Add sugar syrup to orange mixture. Mature for three to four weeks.

Fireplace Logs

Use up your old newspapers and make a colorful fireplace log. Take the newspaper apart, so that you are working with individual, folded-over sheets. Dip the doubled newspaper sheets into a water solution of the chemical and color of your choice according to the list below. You may use sheets of a single color or sheets of various colors to make your log, as desired. Let the pages dry overnight. Take a section of broom handle and coat with soap or spray with silicone (so it will slide out at the end). Wrap the dried page around it tightly, securing the sheet with masking tape. Place a second sheet around the first, again wrapping tightly and securing with masking tape. Repeat the process until the roll is about four inches in diameter. When the last paper is rolled and taped, slide the broom handle out. The log should be ready for burning.

Coloring the Log

The chemicals below may be used on real wood logs, too, either sprinkled on the burning log in powdered form or sprayed on the log in a water solution before it is ignited. Use l oz. of any powder to a gallon of water:

Chemical	Resulting Color
Strontium Nitrate	Red
Table salt	Yellow
Borax	Green
Barium Nitrate	Apple Green
Copper Nitrate	Emerald Green
Calcium Chloride	Orange
Lithium Chloride	Purple
Copper Chloride	Bluish Green

How Do You Clean...

Alabaster

- Clean it just as you clean marble. Use a damp cloth or any detergent heavily diluted with lukewarm water.

Artificial Flowers

- Here's what grandma did: put them in a bag with salt and shake (the bag — not yourself). Take a look at the color of the salt and you'll see what you've accomplished.
- If you douse them with acrylic spray, they'll resist dirt and soil. Get it at craft shops.
- Before you remove the flowers to clean them, in order to remember just how the arrangement was set up, put knitting needles into the spaces where you remove the stems.

Barbecue Kettles

- Make sure kettle is cooled down and wear rubber gloves. Dip a clean cloth into paint thinner and rub the kettle. To clean the grill, use paint thinner applied with a wire brush. Rinse everything thoroughly at the end. Works like a charm, but exercise caution with paint thinner — it's flammable.

Fireplace Grouting

- Smoker's toothpaste applied with a toothbrush does the best job of cleaning the grout around fireplace brick. Don't rinse, just wipe off excess with a damp rag.

Macrame

- Use cold water wash, scrub gently with fingernail brush. Or rub on white cornmeal, then brush off.

Pewter

- To brighten, mix whiting (a chalk) from the hardware with denatured alcohol to make a paste. Apply, let it dry on pewter, then polish. Wash, rinse and dry.
- Or dampen cheesecloth, dip into cigarette ashes. The cheesecloth will turn black as you rub the pewter.

Blinds

- If they're short enough to remove, take them to the car wash, hang them on the wall and give them a good hosing.
- Or put them in the tub under the shower spray.
- Baby wipes are good cleaners.
- Or slip an old sock or glove on your hand, spray with cleaner, and run your hand across the blind.
- An occasional wipe with a fabric softener sheet reduces static, makes dust less likely to accumulate.

Plastic (Resin) Chairs

- Spray with half liquid bleach and half water, wait five minutes, then wipe dry with clean cloth or paper towels.

Stove Knobs and Drip Pans

- Before you tackle the stove, remove all the knobs and drip pans and soak them in a gallon of medium-hot water to which you've added 1/4 cup of dishwasher detergent. When you're finished with the stove, you can rinse the other items clean.

Butcher Block

- Wash, then dry with a cloth; then cover with salt to draw moisture out of the wood.
- But to really remove bacteria, cover it with bleach and salt, scrub it with a stiff brush, then rinse with very hot water and wipe with a clean cloth. Repeat with each use.
- To remove gummy dough, sprinkle salt on a wet sponge and start rubbing. Or use a plastic windshield scraper. It's easier to use than a knife and it won't mark the wood.

The only thing worse than a husband who's handy and won't fix things is a husband who isn't and will.

Refrigerator Coils

- This is the kind of job you can easily forget, but if coils are clogged with dust, your refrigerator will stop working properly. Remove the kick plate at the bottom of your refrigerator and see if the brush attachment of your vacuum will reach underneath. If not, use the cardboard roll from gift wrap as an "extender" to your vacuum. Don't forget to wash the kick plate.

Computer Keyboard

- Vacuum regularly with a soft brush attachment. Occasionally turn the keyboard upside down and pat it sharply — as if you were burping a baby. Dust will be dislodged.
- If there is built-up grime, unplug the computer and use a Q-tip dipped in alcohol on the keys. Water will cause rust, but alcohol evaporates and won't harm keyboard.

Drainboard

- Soak it in bleach and water.
- Coat it with a light film of furniture polish to prevent staining and to make the tray easier to clean.
- Is there a hard water stain? Tilt the low end of the board slightly and pour one cup of white vinegar over the board. Let it set overnight and rub off with a sponge in the morning.

Indoor/Outdoor Carpeting

- Mix a gallon of water, a cup of white vinegar and enough dishwashing soap to make a sudsy solution. Use a brush to scrub it, then blot it dry with bath towels. (Works on indoor rugs, too).

Marble Floor

- The best way is also the easiest. Just wash a marble floor with mild soap and water applied with sponge or mop.

Plastic Model Car Collection

- A dustcloth or a brush might ruin models. Instead, aim a blow dryer to blow away dust; or put them outside, turn hose to "fine spray" and briefly hose them down.

No-Wax Vinyl Floors

- The no-wax shine will last longer if you use a mild cleaner like 1/4 cup of white vinegar to 1 gallon warm water.

Stuffed Toy

- If the tag says "all new materials," a toy can be machine-washed (cold/gentle). If the doll or animal has "hair," put it in a mesh bag or nylon stocking first to protect it. Dry briefly on "air only," then let air dry.
- You can remove a lot of dust from non-washable toys just by putting them in the dryer on "fluff" or "air only". Or shake with a small amount of cornmeal in a plastic garbage bag, then brush clean.

Toaster

- Shine up with club soda or a little ammonia and lots of water.
- Use lighter fluid or nail polish remover to remove plastic that has burned on the toaster and any other electric appliances.

Sheepskin Car Seats

- They can be washed and machine dried on a very low temperature. Remove while still damp and finish by air drying.
- Or wash by hand with Murphy's Oil Soap, use hair conditioner in the rinse to make them fluffy. Dry flat.

Windowsills

- Seeing spots on the sills? Pour a little diluted rubbing alcohol on a soft cloth and rub the surface. The spots will disappear.
- Waxing the window sills will make it easier to clean the grit and dirt off.

A diet thought: leave it on the table
or it will end up on the chair.

If You Can't Stand The Heat

If you feel the need to be alone,
announce you're going to wash the dishes

Angel Food Cakes Don't Rise
- Make sure eggs are room temperature.
- Check to see if there are any pinholes in the pan (if so, replace it) and that there is no residual shortening in the pan.
- Don't flour the pan. Line it with a brown paper grocery bag cut to fit. Don't remove cake from the pan until it is cold.

Cake Layers are Lumpy
- Until I learned this trick, I stuck tiny marshmallows between the layers of my home-made cakes to make them look better, since the bump in the middle was so high, the icing ran down the sides. With this suggestion, I can make the best kind of cake: one that looks as if it came from the bakery but tastes homemade. Wrap a strip of damp terry toweling around the tin before you put it in the oven. Fasten the strip with a safety pin.

Dry Cookies
- Best way to keep cookies moist: Put a piece of fresh bread in the jar.

What's the Beef?
- Meatballs take too long to shape ... so roll the mixture into a long rectangle and slice off chunks. Who says they have to be round?
- Meatloaf cracks ... so rub ice cold water over the top.

Microwave is Dirty
- The easiest way to clean a spill is to cover it with a damp paper towel and turn the oven on high for ten seconds. The mess will wipe up easily when the oven cools.

Liquid has Spilled

- A string mop — the kind you thought was out of fashion, the kind that cartoon wives wave at their husbands when they're mad — is actually better than sponge mops in some circumstances, such as getting under counters and reaching hard to get to areas. Unlike the old-fashioned type, today's string mops can be tossed in the washer and dryer.
- The most effective, fastest spill absorber of all? A disposable diaper!

French Fries aren't Crisp

- Soak cut potatoes in ice water for 15 minutes, dry thoroughly. Fry twice: once for ten minutes, then again when they've cooled. Remove from oil when golden brown.

Mashed Potatoes aren't Smooth

Try any or all of the following:
- Cut in small dice, drain well, make sure the potatoes are well done before mashing, beat them immediately with an electric mixer or a potato ricer.
- Add milk that has been heated first.

One of my readers contributed his personal method of getting lumps out of potatoes: Chew them good, then swallow them!

Iced Tea is Cloudy

- Add a cup of boiling water to the mixture. And next time, add a pinch of baking soda when you make it to prevent cloudiness.

Powdered Iced Tea Cakes

- Keep soda crackers, or part of a slice of bread in the container (same for cookies).
- Keep it in the fridge.
- Put a little bag of rice (in netting, sealed with a rubber band) in the bottle.
- Toothpicks in the jar absorb moisture (and I use this for salt and sugar, too).
- Store it upside down.

Dressing the Salad is Sloppy

- Toss the greens, together with the dressing in the (rinsed out) plastic bag that you carried them home in. Salad will be coated evenly. Better still: No cleanup, no drips.
- If you keep the salad oil in a washed, rinsed margarine squeeze bottle, you can add just a few drops at a time.

Coffee Filters Stick to the Stack

- Take filter from the bottom.
- Blow on the stack.
- Use a small piece of masking tape and touch it to the filter.
- As soon as you've opened the package, turn the stack inside out.
- Hold the package upside down and whack the edges on the counter or table edge several times. They'll fan out, and be easier to separate.

Eggs Crack During Boiling

- Steam them. Once water starts steaming, put eggs in top and turn off heat. Let cook and cool. When you crack shell, eggs will be perfect.

Eggs Are Hard to Peel

- Start them in cold water, heat and boil ten minutes, then plunge into cold water and peel right away.

Disappearing Acts

- Use pieces of uncooked spaghetti instead of toothpicks to skewer rolled-up fish filets or chicken breasts. As the entree cooks, the spaghetti cooks as well. No splinters left in the food.
- If you boil peas in the pods, the heat will burst them open. Peas will sink to the bottom and you can easily skim pods off the top.
- Refrigerate soups — even canned soups — and fat will rise to the top, where it can quickly be removed.

Freezer's a Mess

- Instead of marking the date you put food into the freezer, mark the food with a "use by" date (baked goods 3 months; casseroles 2-3 months; raw meat 4 months; vegetables 8-12 months). You'll be more aware of what you have to use up first.
- Pack fruits and vegetables flat in bags before you freeze them, then "file" them in a plastic or shoe box in your freezer to utilize space better.

Don't Agonize, Improvise:
Subsitutions for the Baker

- Missing an egg and the recipe calls for several? Substitute a teaspoon of cornstarch or a tablespoon of mayonnaise.
- Instead of confectioner's sugar, you can use 1 cup sugar and 1 tablespoon cornstarch.

Ice Cream Crystallizes

- My friend says his mom bought such cheap brands of ice cream that he grew up thinking ice cream was supposed to be crunchy. Personally, I think the problem wasn't the quality of the ice cream but rather the method of storage. After you open the carton, press a piece of plastic wrap or aluminum foil against the surface of the remainder and it will stay creamy and crunchless.

Jar Lid Won't Open

- The simplest solution, to me, is using the tip of an old beer-can opener to pry up the edge slightly; you'll hear a pop as air rushes in to release the vacuum seal. But if jar is stuck because dried food has caked around the top, I reach into my utility drawer for a piece of sandpaper, which makes the best gripper.

Burgers Aren't Done Right

- Some like them rare, some medium — and you're trying to get them all done at the same time! Putting a sliver of ice in the middle of some will keep them nicely underdone while the others cook to medium.

Turkey Never Gets Golden Brown

- The secret to a golden brown turkey is paprika and soy sauce. Rub on some paprika, then pour on a little soy sauce. The bird turns brown even before you put it in the oven. When it's cooked and you bring it out, your table will look like something out of a magazine ad — that is until someone spills the gravy on the tablecloth.

Four Kitchen Items I Couldn't Live Without

- Sharp kitchen shears. I use them to cut pizza, dissect chicken, trim string beans, snip ends off celery and flowers, even cube meat.

- Hand-held mixer. Europeans knew about this long before we did. It's held like a mixer but is strong as a blender. Hold it right in the pot to puree vegetables, blend soups, etc. Much less trouble to clean than a blender.

- Steamer/Spaghetti pot. This is a large pot with two perforated inserts: one shallow, for steaming, and deep one that's great for soup or pasta. You lift it out to to remove bones from stock or drain spaghetti. Sometimes I use both inserts together: vegetables on top, noodles on bottom. When all are cooked, I add sauce for a one-dish meal.

- Small food processor: Great for making a small amount of chopped nuts, minced onion, parsley. I use it for grating carrots and celery for meatloaf. In fact, because it's compact, I keep it out all the time and hardly ever use the big food processor.

I believe no dish should take more than 30 minutes to prepare, unless someone else is cooking it.

Boiling Pointers

- To avoid boil-away: Keep a few marbles or pebbles in the bottom of your double boiler. They'll rattle when the water gets low and remind you to refill it.
- To avoid boilover: Rub an inch or two of fat or oil around the top of the pot and starchy dishes such as rice and pea soup won't bubble over.

Shedding Less Tears When Chopping Onions

- Refrigerate them before chopping.
- Peel them under cold, running water.
- Keep your mouth tightly closed while chopping.
- Wear glasses.
- Or chop at the stove with exhaust fan running.
- Or wear a diving mask.

Garlic Hints

Garlic, somebody said is the ketchup of intellectuals. Ever since I heard that one I've been serving lots of dishes that have garlic in them. But unless you've got a lot of time to kill, you could go crazy peeling those tiny little cloves.

- Take a drinking glass and bang it down on the head of cloves. Then take each individual clove and bang the glass down again. They slip right out of there.
- To remove garlic odor from hands, just rub them in a handful of used coffee grounds, lemon juice or vinegar. I've been told in Italy, that if you eat a whole coffee bean after a garlic-rich meal, your lover will find you desirable again. My luck, the meal would put him to sleep.

It's A Wash

Doing laundry is the great equalizer. I don't think I've met anyone who hasn't had an occasional personal encounter with a washing machine. It's the subject I get the most mail about. And here are some of the most interesting items I've collected.

A Refresher Course in Things Your Mother Told You About Stain Removal, But You've Forgotten. (She was Right.)

- Blot up the spill thoroughly before you try to remove a stain.
- Act quickly and you'll have the best chance of removing a stain. Something that's been washed and thrown in the dryer may be a problem. Dryer heat may set a stain.
- Test any solution in a hidden area to make sure it doesn't create yet another stain.
- Apply water or stain-removal solution to the stained spot only, using an eye-dropper or a bottle with a small pouring spout. Otherwise you'll spread the stain.
- When sponging off a stain, work inward.
- A heavy glass pie plate, turned upside down, makes a good working surface for removing stains from fabric.

Feeling Pressed? Then Skip the Ironing ...

- Take a shirt right out of the washing machine, put it on a hanger, and spritz some spray starch on the cuffs and collar, then let it hang dry. It will look so good that only the fussiest person would demand that the shirt actually come in contact with an iron.
- Wet handkerchiefs thoroughly, then flatten on a smooth surface to dry.
- Hang damp, drip-dry shirts on hangers, then spray collars and cuffs with spray starch. No ironing needed.
- Your husband likes creases in his jeans? Tell him to put them between the mattress and bed — and sleep on it. Rather, on them.
- For years, I ironed my triple pleated sheers. That one day — voila! — I hung them damp. Guess what? They looked great.
- Your little girl's hair ribbons will look fine if you pull them over a hot toaster or lightbulb — or through a curling iron.
- Hang a tie in the bathroom when your husband is showering. If he loves a steamy shower, the wrinkles should come out of his tie with no problem.

Shrunken Sweater

I've had reports of success resizing a sweater with each of these solutions.
- Soak sweater in hair conditioner and water solution, pull gently to reshape.
- Or dissolve one oz. Borax in a couple of tablespoons of hot water, add mixture to a gallon of lukewarm water, immerse garment, pull gently into shape, and rinse in a gallon of warm water to which you add 2 tablespoons vinegar.
- Or dissolve one or two cups non-iodized salt in enough hot water to cover garment. Let cool, and leave sweater to soak for three hours. Wash it in mild suds, rinse three times, spin or roll sweater in towels.

Overdried Clothes

- If you have wrinkles because wash and wear clothes were left too long in the dryer, just put them back in with a damp towel and run a cycle on warm. Or press the item with a pressing clothing dampened with white distilled vinegar (straight or diluted with water).

Limp Curtains

- To the final rinse water, add one of the following: 1 cup dry milk, 1/2 cup liquid starch, or 1 cup Epsom salts (then turn last rinse to wash and wear cycle)

Stone-Washing Your Jeans

I get so many requests for this information that I include it here for reference.

- Saturate an old towel with a half-and-half mix of bleach and water and toss it in the dryer with the jeans. Run on "high" for 15-20 minutes. Or mist with bleach in a spray bottle.
- Or mix a thin paste of automatic dishwasher detergent and water in a plastic bowl, using a wooden spoon. With a paint-brush, spread mixture unevenly onto surface of jeans that have been laid flat on an old plastic sheet. Do other side of jeans, leave for 3-4 hours, wash as usual and dry.
- Or squirt liquid Cascade at random over the jeans, turn shower to hot and spray jeans until Cascade has blended into denim. Let stand for 10-15 minutes, repeat on other side. Put jeans carefully into garbage bag when completed and transfer them to washing machine. Wash without soap on regular cycle.

The height of elegance was the woman who had her money ironed.
As for me, I'm just pressed for money.

If Laundry is 'Stiff'

- Many people complain that their towels and other items come out stiff. This is the case because some soapy water always remains in the machine drain hose and mixes with the rinse water. Extra rinse cycles will help — use hand-held extension on the faucet for the final rinse. Also cut down on the soap or detergent by as much as 3/4.

- Or add a commercial rinse agent or white vinegar to first rinse. Remove smell of vinegar with Downy or 1/4 cup baking soda in final rinse, if necessary.

Board of Directions

A bulletin board in the washroom can be a great reference "library."

- Use it to keep new household hints for laundry that you have clipped from a magazine or newspaper (maybe even from my column!). You'll refer to it from time to time, then it will become part of your routine and you can toss it away. (You can use the same idea in the kitchen).

- Post cleaning instructions for special clothing items. (Some people prefer using a 3x5 card file but I don't have that many instructions to keep track of. If care instructions are too complicated — I don't buy the item!)

- You can also use the bulletin board to keep buttons, snaps, and threaded needles handy for repairs so they'll be done right away.

Marked Down

- It's really annoying to put a stained item through the wash without pretreating it, because often the result is that you set in the stain. To prevent such a thing, ask your family to tie a loose knot in any piece of item that needs special treating before they throw it into the hamper . You can use a safety pin to mark the spot yourself (on such items as tablecloths). The easiest solution for me is to use a disappearing fabric marker to circle the spots if I plan to do the laundry within a day or so.

Liquid Dish Soap Does More Than Dishes

- You can give your most precious hand-washable luxury care for only pennies. Just add one or two squirts of liquid dish detergent (I prefer Palmolive Dishwashing Liquid) to a sink full of water (6 or 7 squirts to a laundry tub), then soak your items for three minutes and rinse. Items will be gently cleaned — and also soft and smelling sweet.
- Remove the soil mark around the collar by applying dish soap with a small paint brush or an old toothbrush. Then launder the garment as usual.

Dry Ideas

- Reset your machine for an extra spin-dry when you have a heavy load, and you won't need to keep items in the dryer as long or on as high a temperature.
- To make down fluffier, throw a pair of clean tennis shoes into the dryer with it or drop several racquet balls into socks and add them to the machine.
- Install a towel rack on the ceiling directly over the center of the bathtub. You can hang several items to dry at the same time and the water drips neatly into the tub.
- Clothing that has been stored for the summer may be tossed into the dryer along with a fabric softener sheet to get rid of any musty odor. Set the dryer on "air", and leave the item inside for just a few minutes. Same treatment works to dust items like drapes.

Handling With Care

- It's better to wash delicate items by hand, of course, but you don't get the agitation action of a machine, which gets things really clean. You can simulate it by drilling several holes in a small rubber plunger, putting the clothes in a small basin, then plunging away.
- Or use your salad spinner as a mini washing machine.

Just Kidding

Labor is Nature's way of preparing you for motherhood.
Afterwards, nothing seems out of the question.

Baby Stuff

Wash and Care

- If you find bathing your newborn is a little scary, wear thin cotton gloves. You'll get a better grip.
- Use a latticework plastic laundry basket as a minitub inside your bathtub for an infant who is able to sit. The water flows through and the baby won't slide around.

Feeding Time

- Slip a sock over the baby's bottle. It will feel soft to the baby and warm his hands.
- Personalize your baby's bottles (with a dab of nail polish) so when she gets together with other children, you'll know which of the dropped bottles is hers!
- Carry sweater clips with you for those times when you need to improvise a bib out of a restaurant napkin. Or slip a couple of extra safety pins on your key ring for that purpose.

Getting Organized

- A towel rack fastened to the end of the crib is the perfect place to hang the crib blanket. And a bicycle basket at the other end can hold diaper changing supplies now and pajamas later.
- A mirror hung next to the changing table keeps the baby amused while you're working on him.
- Use a calendar for jotting down your infant's "first" — you may not have time right away to record them in the baby book.
- Stash a combination lock in the diaper bag to secure the baby's stroller to a railing if you must leave it unattended while you take her into a restaurant or shop.
- Make up the baby's bed with two sets of sheets and pads, with a rubber-backed flannel sheet in between. If he just wets the bed, it's easier to strip off one layer only than to make the bed from scratch.

Dressing Up

- Hate putting a long-sleeved shirt on a little one who is waving his fingers around? Slip a pair of baby socks over his little hands first. Give an older child a small ball and let him hold it until you've poked the arm through, then transfer the ball to the other hand.
- Snaps on jeans will close easier if the inside is coated with a drop of petroleum jelly or non-stick vegetable spray.

Everyday and Special Days

All Washed Up

- Toothpaste removes a Kool-Aid mustache quickly and tastes better than soap if some gets in your mouth.
- Bathtime will be safer if you always turn the cold water faucet off last so there won't be any hot drips.
- Make a bath seem more appealing by offering frozen juice pops as a treat. Drips are no problem, either! And you'll cut down protests at shampoo time if you make that more fun. Create"ears" and "horns" out of lathered hair, and have a mirror handy so kids may admire themselves.
- Float the shampoo bottle in the warm tub water before you wash your child's hair; the soap won't feel so cold on her scalp.
- To keep shampoo out of a child's eyes, let him wear plastic swim goggles, or have him lie back, with his head supported by a small plastic "life preserver."
- If your child is a bedwetter, save your mattress by slipping an old, clean shower curtain between the pad and the mattress

Party Time

- For a first birthday, skip the cake and spread a plastic dropcloth on the floor. In the middle, place an unbreakable tray filled with kiddy hors d'oeuvres such as cubes of pear and soft cheese, slivers of avocado, cereal, biscuits and pretzels. Let the kids at it — and be sure to have some cameras around.
- The night before a birthday, when your child is asleep, decorate his room with balloons — a special way to start a special day.

Clothes Encounters

Foot Notes

- When the soles of sleepers with feet wear through, cut them off and use the pieces as a pattern to crochet a replacement. Attach them to the feet of the sleeper with a buttonhole stitch.
- The ribbed portions of adult sports socks make cozy leg warmers for little ones. Protect the legs of babies at the crawling stage with the ribbed portion of tube socks. You might want to tape a couple of gauze squares at the knee to give baby extra protection.
- If you make two small slits in the tongue of a shoe and pull the shoelaces through the slits as you lace the shoes, the tongues won't curl and press into the child's feet.
- Leftover yarn or thin ribbon can serve as emergency shoelaces.

Dealing with Hangups

- If two kids are sharing a closet, use different-color hangers to separate the clothes.
- An expansion plant pole makes a good coat rack because it can be adjusted to various heights.

Right at Hand

- Mittens keep the hand warmer than gloves. Find a style of mitten your child likes and that fits well. Then buy three pairs in the same style and color. You'll always have a match.
- Sew a mitten clip to the lining at the hem of your child's ski jacket to hold a knitted cap so it can dry after use and be right at hand the next day.
- Velcro strips attached to both sleeves of a coat and to mittens will keep them from going astray. (And you can use the same idea with the scarf.)

Patch Work

- Prolong the life of kids' activewear (and your own) by patching garments on the wrong side before they're worn. Reinforce knees of jeans with iron-on interfacing. Sweater elbows can be pre-patched with squares of nylon pantyhose. The nylon is sheer, so it's not visible, but it's very strong.

- Let the kids wear soccer kneepads while they play and the knees of the sweatpants won't wear out as quickly. Bonus: knees won't get scraped as often.
- A small run in a little girl's fancy tights can be repaired with a length of satin ribbon sewn to the spot. Add a little button or bow.

Disciplinary Action

Device-ive Actions

- Better than reminding your child when it's time to come in: Buy her an alarm wristwatch, or tell her she can play outside until she spots the first firefly of the evening.

- Use the kitchen timer to end quarrels about whose turn it is for tasks and treats. Tell the kids that when the timer rings, it's time to switch. You can also use a timer to sound a bedtime warning or set a limit on dressing/undressing time.

- Your toddler may allow you some uninterrupted phone time if you hand her a toy phone for her own use while you talk. (Hide her phone away and pull it out for just such occasions.)

- One way to stop those interminable discussions about whose turn it is: Let them throw a set of dice. The high roller "loses."

Making Points

- Hang a bulletin board on an older child's closed door. Leave messages and instructions on it instead of having to knock. He may respond more enthusiastically.

- If nothing else works, try a point system for enforcing various rules (picking up clothes, clearing the table). So many points are necessary to win various privileges — such as TV watching, visiting the comic store.

- Make a "lost and found" for shoes, toys, books, etc. and charge the children to retrieve their lost possessions.

Wet and Not Wild

A nursery-school teacher told me that one of the best ways to soothe an out-of-sorts child is with water play. Fill the tub and add toys. If you haven't bubble bath, add some baby shampoo. And a touch of food coloring will make it even more fun. (Don't worry — it won't stain.)

Getting Dressed

- If children (and you) lay out clothes the night before, you can save lots of time in the morning.

- Kids will get the correct shoe on the appropriate foot if you make a mark — such as a red nail-polish dot — inside each shoe and show the youngsters how to set down the pair of shoes so the dots are together. Or paint a big toe on the sole of each in order to show young children which shoe goes on which foot.

- Zipper pulls on snowsuits and jackets are a cinch to deal with if you hang a trinket from the end. A disk reflector made for pet wear, attached with a lanyard hook, is perfect. Or use a metal key ring.
- To keep backpack from slipping, thread the strap through the first part of the buckle. Then twist the strap once or twice. Continuing threading the rest of the strap through the buckle.
- Tell little ones to button shirts and coats from the bottom up, so the buttons will come out even at the top.

Laces in Place

Tying shoelaces: They will stayed tied better if they're dampened before you do it.
Untying shoelaces: Use the prong of a fork inserted into the knot to loosen it.

Table Manners

- Candy and cookies that have been frozen are nice in hot weather and also easier to eat — less crumbling
- If you have no baby seat but the restaurant has stackable chairs, stack several to create your own "high chair."
- In a restaurant, ask that children's drinks be served in paper cups with lids and straws. You'll save time wiping up spills.
- Little ones can practice drinking from a cup while they're in the tub. Spills are no problem. (But make sure they don't drink the bath water!)

Best Foot Forward

The person who said if the shoe fits, wear it, obviously has never taken a look at my son's tennis shoes. Here are a few hints for shoe care:

- If you spray canvas tennis shoes with spray starch or a fabric protector when they're clean, they'll stay white longer.
- Clean white leather sneakers with white wall tire cleaner.

Well and Good

- Having children suck on an ice cube or an ice pop before they swallow a bad-tasting medicine will numb their taste buds.

- A thermal jug at the bedside keeps a cool drink handy when a child needs to spend the day in bed.

- When you've a toddler, keep juice-flavored ice cubes on hand in the freezer. If your little one bumps his lip, sucking on a juice-flavored ice cube will reduce the swelling. And buy a red washcloth to clean up bumps and scrapes. Not seeing blood makes your child calmer.

- Kids tend to gag when you use a tongue depresser on them. Try a flat lollipop instead.

- Children's sunglasses aren't very effective at blocking ultra-violet rays. Trim adult clip-ons to snap onto children's frames.

- Use a three-minute egg timer to show a child how long she should brush her teeth.

- It's so easy to forget details about growing children, so keep a medical diary. Record visits to the doctor, allergic reactions to any prescriptions, dates of shots, heights and weights. It's practical and sometimes even fun to look back on, too.

To a mom, the handwriting on the wall isn't a sign that something bad will happen. It's a sign that something bad has already happened.

Out Of A Pickle

When a reader one day asked what could be done with leftover pickle juice, I turned to my readers for help. Hundreds of letters poured in, which goes to show how creative folks can be! I found it inspiring if not actually awesome. Here are the best of the lot.

Uses for Sweet Pickle Juice

Meat

- Brown pork chops, drain off fat, add pickle juice and cover. Cook till brown on both sizes. This tenderizes and glazes the chops.
- Baste a ham with cloves, mustard and pickle juice.
- Add juice to meatloaf.
- Add leftover boned chicken to the juice plus some vinegar and sugar.
- Try it on back bacon to give it a little zip.
- Grind leftover or deli ham, cut green pepper and celery fine, stir in some pickle relish and pickle juice for a no-mayonnaise ham salad.
- Or marinate uncooked chicken in pickle juice plus Dijon mustard and garlic; drain, bake at 350 for 45 minutes, basting every 15 minutes.
- Make sweet and sour meatball gravy: 1-2 cups pickle juice, juice of two fresh lemons, 1/4 cup chili sauce or ketchup, plus any meatball mixture. If you want a thicker gravy, five minutes before serving mix 2 tablespoons of cornstarch with 1/2 cup water and pour into mixture. Stir until absorbed.
- Make brisket of beef with juice plus a package of onion soup mix and a package of mushroom soup mix. Cover with aluminum foil and bake at 300° for three hours (similar to sour-bratten gravy).
- Or, after browning roast, pour sweet pickle juice over meat, simmer for a couple of hours, covered, till done.
- Simmer deli pastrami slices in it, serve on rye with mustard.
- Marinate steak in pickle juice.

Vegetables

- Whip juice with cream cheese and use as a dip for vegetables (or chips).
- Keep it in a salt shaker to use on lettuce and tomato salad.

- Season hot cooked broccoli or cooked cauliflower with pickle juice (fewer calories than added butter or cheese).
- Use juice in all mayonnaise dressings.
- Make pickled peppers by cutting strips of red and green pepper, adding juice, sealing and leaving for two weeks.
- Or put sliced zucchini in the jar.
- Cook small frozen onions and put them in the juice for two to three days.
- Or pickle fresh and/or canned beets.
- Cook green beans in pickle juice, add bacon or slivered almonds.
- Chop bell peppers and add to sweet pickle juice; serve on lettuce salad.
- Slice red or yellow onions thin, place in jars, boil your juice and pour over. In a few days, you have delicious onions.
- Add juice to paper-thin slices of cucumber and onion rings, plus some dill and sour cream.
- Drain jarred pimento and pour pickle juice over; pimento won't mold.
- Shred cabbage, cook it in bacon fat, add some pickle juice.

Other kitchen ideas

- Sweet pickle juice can be added to potato salad, tuna salad, stew (midway through cooking) and cottage cheese with finely chopped bell pepper, scallion.
- Put sliced dills in sweet pickle juice to get sweet dills.
- Use juice for pickling cucumber or to marinate coarsely chopped onion overnight to use on salads, hot dogs, etc.
- Use juice to replace 2/3 of cold water when making vegetable salad with lemon or lime gelatin.
- Make pickled eggs by heating juice to boiling, then adding shelled, hard cooked eggs (allow to cool, store in fridge).
- Add juice to homemade soups or spaghetti sauce.
- Take a sip when you have an upset stomach.
- Add a tablespoon of juice plus horseradish and lemon to a cup of mayonnaise for tartar sauce.
- Juice is a great addition to cole slaw.
- Mix sour cream, a bit of sugar and juice to make creamed cucumbers.
- Cornbread salad: Prepare and bake 1 box corn muffin mix as bread in square pan. When cool, crumble into bits. Chop 3

green peppers, 1 large onion, 4 tomatoes, 1/4 cup dill or sweet pickles, and crumble 2 pounds of cool, crisp, cooked bacon. Layer the bread, bacon, and vegetables, sprinkle with salt and pepper, then sprinkle on pickles plus 1/4 cup sweet pickle relish. Combine 1 cup mayonnaise, 1/2 cup pickle juice (dill or sweet), 1 tablespoon sugar. Drizzle over salad. Toss before serving. May be made one day in advance.
- Use juice to make mincemeat.

As a house cleaner
- Keeps drains clean and sweet.
- Use in bathtub, basin and kitchen sink.
- Clean burned-on food off grills and iron skillets: get them hot, pour juice on, simmer for 5 minutes and rinse.
- Juice cleans Paul Revere pots and pans with copper bottoms.

And for the garden
- Great for gardenia bushes at least once a year.
- Azelea bushes also thrive on juice.

Uses for Dill Pickle Juice

- Combine with finely shredded purple cabbage.
- Cut carrots matchstick shape and put them in dill pickle juice.
- Or combine juice with fresh spears of cucumber.
- Also good for large diced pieces of celery.
- Use it to pickle baby mushrooms.
- Drain a can of beans (waxed or green) and put them in the dill juice as a good side dish.
- Salt and pepper a roast beef, top with dill pickle juice and slices of dill pickle, cook in slow cooker until it falls apart; mash it together, serve on buns.

Outta Here

Home remedies (mostly non-toxic) to get rid of unwelcome pests

Ants

- If you've got ants in your pantry, sprinkle some whole cloves around the floor, and in the corners of cupboards. Dried coffee grounds outside the house turn them away, too. And so does cinnamon.
- When you're feeding Fido outdoors, put his bowl in a shallow bowl of water (about 1" in diameter larger than the feeding bowl). The ants will fall into the "moat" before they can reach his food.

Barnacles

- If they're attaching themselves to your boat, add a good dose of cayenne pepper to the paint can next time you repaint the hull and the barnacles will reattach elsewhere.

Bats (in the attic)

- Hang mothballs in a porous bag; or burn sulphur candles.
- Seal, caulk or weatherstrip all openings more than 1/4 wide except one, then wait three days; half an hour after dark (when they're out feeding) seal last hole. If one comes in, open doors or widows and turn off all lights and it will fly out.
- If they're roosting in porch eaves, tack up heavy plastic sheeting around walls so they have nothing to hang onto.

Bee Stings

- Scrape the stinger out right away with a sharp knife as if you're shaving. (Don't use tweezers. They squeeze more venom into your system.)
- Use a baking soda paste (for itching) and ice (for swelling). Caution: If there is severe swelling or a rash, see a doctor. Some people are fatally allergic to bee stings.

Beetles

- To discourage Japanese beetles, plant regular spring onions or garlic.
- Dust rose bushes with self-rising flour and you'll smother the beetles.
- Our county extension service recommended Rocky Spore Disease (from the nursery) that will kill the grub worms and eventually, the beetles. Beetles on rose bushes can be dispelled with Diazinon but worms have to go first.

Birds

- It's very sad when birds build their nests around the air conditioning units because the heat prevents the babies from surviving. Try placing a big-eyed stuffed animal at the window to discourage birds from nesting.
- Any kind of noisemaker, particularly a bright one, discourages birds. You can make a noisemaker from empty can lids hung from strings with knots in between.
- Or use Christmas tinsel garlands attached to a porch column or a TV antenna.
- Kids' toy pinwheels stuck in a windowbox will keep birds away, too.
- Or try mothballs hung in a bag made from an old stocking.

Box Elder Bugs

- Spray with water and dishwashing detergent (about 8 parts water to 1 part detergent). Mixture won't hurt shrubbery.

Crickets

- Find the area where they enter and put a length of tape on it, sticky side up. Turn ends under to keep tape in place. When the crickets go to the spot, they will get stuck. You can remove them safely.
- Boric acid kills not only roaches and silverfish, but also crickets.
- If you don't have pets or children around, leave crushed mothballs around the outside foundation and doors. They won't jump through mothballs because the substance would stick on their legs and be harmful. (Repeat when mothballs dissolve.) Inside, you can sprinkle mothballs behind stoves, refrigerators, and beds.
- Raid sprayed on garbage keeps them away.

Deer

- Mix l cup milk, 2 eggs, 2 T. liquid detergent and 2 T. cooking oil into 2 gallons of water and spray plants.
- Or mix l8 raw eggs with 5 gallons of water (enough for one acre). The scent offends deer, is too weak to bother humans.
- Or use dried blood from the garden store.

Dogs and Cats, Visiting

- Spray the garbage pails with pine scented cleaner.
- One or more glass or plastic gallon-sized cartons filled 2/3 with water will keep dogs away. If they pass by the containers, put out more bottles placed closer together.
- Put fir boughs around shrubs where cats leave their mark. They like to cover up after themselves, and since boughs will prevent this, they'll stay away. The boughs also protect plants from winter cold and are a non-toxic solution.

Dogs and Cats, Indoors

- Keep cats out of the planters by putting clothespins in the soil, about 6" apart.
- Cats will stay away from a furniture leg that's been wiped with chili sauce and blotted thoroughly. You can't smell it — but the cat can. Or try liniment.
- Oil of cloves rubbed onto table legs seems to deter puppies.
- Keep cats out of houseplants by making a doughnut shaped cheesecloth cover with a hole big enough for the stem, stitch up the inside circle, and use elastic thread for the outer circle so it fits over the pot. Watering through the cloth is no problem. Or cut a hole for the stem, then cover the soil with a plastic saucer.
- Pine cones or horticultural charcoal will keep the cat's paws away, too.

Gophers

- Put carbide powder down the holes, pour water over it, cover it with a plastic sheet and weight it down. Have all needed items ready before you start and have them conveniently within reach.
- Put a tablespoon of peanut butter at the entrance of the hole, put a small slice of onion and a dab of peanut butter on the gopher trap. With this, a friend caught five a day.

Insects, Indoor

- Mix 1/4 cup Ivory to a gallon of water and spray it on house plants. The bugs like soap about as much as your little kid does.

Mice

- Place hedge apples from the garden in the area where they gather.

Mosquitos

- Don't wear fragrance, eat less sugar (mosquitoes attack people who eat a lot of sugar).
- Or try a cucumber cube: Peel cucumbers, strain them, freeze the liquid in ice cube trays and rub cubes on face and hands.
- A dab of Ultra Brite relieves itching.

Moths (In cupboard):

- Non-toxic solutions: bay leaves, chewing gum, cloves.

Moths (in closet)

- Camphor cakes are preferred by some because after the garment is taken from the storage bag, odor is dispelled in air.

Raccoons

- If they're raiding the garbage, sprinkle cayenne pepper around the cans.

Roaches and Waterbugs

- Don't bring them along when you move: Sprinkle moth balls in each carton.
- Closing drains at night (cover even shower drain), and spraying bug spray into the kitchen sink drain may find you bug-free when nothing else has worked.
- A friend allergic to bug spray zaps water bugs with a shot of rubbing alcohol from a spray bottle. They shrivel up and die.

- Mix equal parts powdered sugar and borax or boric acid crystals. Leave in containers (but not where children or pets can get to it!)
- Or a strong pesticide followed by boric acid compound sprinkled in cupboard corners, floor cracks, etc. (Not near kids or pets, though!)

Snakes

- Get a bag of sulphur at the feed store or garden store and sprinkle it around house and lawn. Will keep ants away, too.

Wasps

- Make a sugar water solution in a small, covered margarine tub, make a small hole, hang in a tree where they'll crawl in and won't get out.

Pet Subjects

Making a Gesture

- About 3/4 of pet owners celebrate their pets' birthdays. Instead of buying a present for your own well-loved pooch or pussy-cat, how about making a donation to the SPCA or Humane Society?

Bird Feed

- Funnel seed into an empty salt box and you'll be able to fill the small cups in your pet's cage neatly.
- A large shower cap makes an excellent birdseed catcher for the bottom of the cage. It fits snugly, washes easily, and is less expensive than ones you buy.

Flight Controller

- When trying to recapture an escaped bird, throw a small, lightweight towel over it when it lands. You reduce the chance of injuring the bird, which can happen if you keep clutching at it with your hands.

On the Collar

- Write your name and phone number on your pet's flea collar. (Shows up best on a white one). And while you're at it, write the date it was purchased. You'll be able to check whether it's time to buy a new one.
- If you put reflector tape on your pet's collar, it will be safer when crossing streets at night.

Catch and Carry

- Use a laundry basket as a pet carrier. Then, for a handle, use twist-ties or elastic bands tied to one another. The animal can see where she's going and you can easily disinfect the basket after the trip.
- Or use an empty disposable diaper box. The built-in handle comes in handy. Just be sure to make air holes and tape the door closed for the trip.

Dry Shampoo

- If your cat needs a bath (due to an accident) but won't stand for a dunking, try rubbing a small amount of corn meal into his fur, then brush it out. The meal absorbs dirt and oils (and I use the same technique to clean fur collars of coats!)

Chow Time

- Cats may leave the dry food in the bowl, hoping for some that's freshly poured. However, a light sprinkle of water may bring out the scent in the dry food and make it tempting again.
- When you pour the oil off the tuna, give a little to your kitty. Oil in their diets prevents furballs.
- Glue a rubber ring to the bottom of the dish, or feed your pet with one of those baby bowls with suction cups to prevent the bowl from moving around.

In the Dog House

- If your pet prefers the outdoors in cold weather, line his favorite box or resting place with aluminum foil. The foil will reflect the animal's body heat and keep him just a bit warmer.
- Want an entrance "door" for the dog house? Make it out of a piece of indoor/outdoor carpeting cut to size, slit up the middle, and nailed in place. An old rubber floor mat serves this purpose as well. Guide your dog through the flap a few times until he has learned how to do it himself.

Dog Days

- Buy a kiddie pool for your dog to splash in so she can refresh herself in the heat of summer.
- You'll keep Fido from overturning his outdoor water bowl if you fasten an angel-food cake pan in place with a stake through the center, then fill with water.

New Dog, New Tricks

- Hang a bell from the door. When you take a new puppy outside, give it a ring. The dog will learn to ring it himself when he has to go out.
- To discourage aggressive begging, grab the dog by the scruff of the neck, force him down for a minute or two, then release and ignore him briefly.

Grooming

- A baby brush or a lint brush makes a nice soft brush for the cat. You can remove loose hairs...and your cat will probably love the stroking.
- Before combing out a long–haired dog, rub some baby powder into his coat.
- Rubbing a fabric softener sheet on a dog's fur cuts static electricity.
- Add a tablespoon of baby oil to the final rinse when you wash your dog. And put the rinse in a watering can with a sprinkler. It's gentle.
- Vet bills are high for nail trimming, but if your pet has learned to scratch on the cabinet where you keep his treats, you've got an easy solution. Using masking tape, fasten sandpaper where the dog scratches. It saves the cabinet finish and manicures nails at the same time.

Litter Manners

- Make inexpensive liners out of 30-gallon garbage bags. Cut them in half across the width. The bottom makes one liner. Seam the opening on the top half with a plastic bag sealer to make a second liner.
- The best way to deodorize a litter box is to leave it outdoors for a few days. Do not use cleaners containing phenol (such as Lysol). They are poisonous to cats.

Accident Insurance

- If your puppy has wet the rug, try this: Sprinkle a cup of cat box filler on the area and press down so it can absorb all the moisture. Let it stand for a couple of hours...then sweep clean.

Dogs on the Trail

- If your pet strays while you're on vacation, an ID tag with your home phone number is of little value if no one is home to answer a call. Replace the tag (or add a second ID) with the phone number of a friend who knows your itinerary.
- When he's along for a lengthy car ride, your pet may get thirsty too. Start the trip with a plastic freezer container full of frozen water. As it thaws, he'll have a fresh water supply.

Hair Removal

- Rub hair on upholstery with a facial sponge "scrubber".
- Or run a damp sponge mop over carpeting (or a large sponge over upholstery) in between (or before) vacuuming.
- Or wipe upholstery with a rag dipped in warm water and then wrung out.
- Try putting a throw rug on the couch and see if your pet will make that the bed. And spray a static-preventor on furniture and clothes to repel hairs.

I think the phrase "man's best friend" was obviously created before wall-to-wall carpeting was invented.

Taking Care of You

For 'Natural' Beauties

- Spearmint: Boil one quart of water with four teaspoons of spearmint leaves. When cooked, this is a great after shampoo rinse for oily hair.
- Tea: Is a fine natural rinse.
- Strawberries: A toothbrush dipped in mashed berries and used briskly on your teeth can remove yellowing and stains.
- Cucumbers: Slices of cold cucumber applied to your eyelids will help banish redness and puffiness

Braces Brighteners

I've had people write to tell me that they were wearing those new braces — made of a new type of plastic — that get stained from coffee, tea and smoking. The dentist I consulted recommends mixing baking soda and hydrogen peroxide to the consistency of yogurt and applying the mixture to your teeth — but not to your gum tissue — with a soft bristled brush. If it burns, dilute the mixture with water. Repeat daily for 10-14 days and you should see improvement.

- And if you're worried that your braces will show in photographs, here's a tip the models use: rub a bit of petroleum jelly on them (it'll refract the light). And rub the jelly off after the photo session.

Bathing and Showering

- A terry cloth dishtowel is a fine substitute for a bath brush when it comes to sloughing off dead skin.
- Add a little shampoo to the bathwater and there'll be no tub ring.
- Put your body lotion in the microwave for 30-45 seconds before you shower. It's much more pleasant to rub on.

Combs and Brushes

- You'll see combs sparkle with little effort if you spray them on both sides with a foam bathroom cleaner, let set briefly, and rinse them off.
- Clean your hair brush with a grout brush. The long, hard bristles reach the base where soil collects.

Deodorant

- If it's gotten "used up" but there's plenty left at the bottom of the container, melt it in a pan, pour it into a single tube and leave it to harden in the refrigerator.

Eyebrows

- How now, unruly brow! If you want your brows to stay in place — dab a bit of styling mousse or hair spray on an old toothbrush and use it to shape them.
- A layer of loose powder on your brow helps you see hairs better when you're tweezing.
- If you're using regular tweezers, treat yourself to a new pair that has a scissors-type handle; it's much easier to work with.
- When your tweezers are starting to lose their grip — give them a rub with sand paper or an emery board.

Those Eyes ...

- Need a "smudger" to soften the edge of eyebrow pencil or liner? Use a clean rubber eraser.
- Using dark mascara on your top lashes and light mascara on the bottom ones will minimize dark circles under your eyes.

Those Lips ...

- Petroleum jelly in an empty lipstick tube becomes portable lip gloss. If you add a bit of leftover lipstick, you'll have tinted gloss.
- Your lips will stay kissable if you apply ChapStick at least 5 times a week. It helps hold the lipstick too.
- Use a lip-coloring pencil on your entire lips and you won't need a touch-up for hours.

Splinters

- If you put a drop of iodine on the splinter, it'll be easier to spot for removing with tweezers.
- Or put a bit of rubber cement or white glue on the spot, let it dry, and pull it away. It will take the splinter along with it.

Hair Care

- Use distilled water instead of conditioning liquid in your mist setter. It will hold your set just as well as the conditioner.
- If you have too much buildup from repeated use of hair spray, gel or mousse, try this trick that was passed along to me from a professional: make a paste of shampoo and a little baking soda, lather, and wash again.
- Being out of cream rinse doesn't mean you're out of luck. Just try a dab of fabric softener in a glass of warm water. it leaves hair soft … and snarl-free.

- You probably already know the trick for a dry shampoo — cornstarch or baby powder sprinkled on and then brushed out. But if you want to do a really great job of removing dirt and oils, put a stocking over the bristles and continue to brush. This will clean your hair and restore the sheen.
- Give your hair instant body by dissolving gelatin in warm water and mixing it with your favorite shampoo.

Dyeing

- Before putting henna or color on your hair, coat the sink lightly with liquid dishwashing detergent. No more sink stains!
- Skin around the hairline stained from your tint? Try rubbing leftover tint into the stained area, then rinsing with water. And next time, put some petroleum jelly around the hairline, ears and neck before you start.
- If you color your hair, summer activities or vacation plans may keep you away from the beauty salon longer than usual. In between visits, use cotton swabs to touch up.
- If there's dye remaining on your face after the application, here's the surprising solution; mix some water with cigarette ashes, apply and—like magic—you'll have no stains and no redness. Just wipe away. The only problem you may have is coming up with a smoker, these days!

Color Problems

- Bleached hair may turn orange if your water contains dissolved and invisible iron called "clear iron." The cheapest solution is soaking your hair with a lot of lemon juice — maybe two lemons' worth — and leaving it on for an hour or so.
- And if your hair has turned green in the pool, use a tomato juice rinse.

---

*The exercise that really changes your life
is walking down the aisle.*

Home Permanents

- Wind a doubled-over tube sock around your forehead and fasten it with a clothespin or another non-magnetic clip. It'll catch drips while your permanent is taking.

- Sponge rollers instead of waving paper are easier to work with and can give you a looser set.

- When giving yourself a permanent wave, apply neutralizer from a pump spray bottle for a good all-over application.

- If your hands stick to those plastic gloves, apply a light dusting of baby powder to your hands. It will absorb any perspiration and your hands will slip right in - and out.

- If you haven't a plastic cape that the directions call for, use a plastic garbage bag that you can toss away.

Hands

- To clean greasy hands, squirt shaving cream in one hand, sprinkle sugar on the other, rub briskly and wash.

- Before you do dirty work in the garden or elsewhere, spray on non-stick vegetable oil and rub it in until it disappears — like hand cream.

- To soften your hands, pour a tablespoon of olive oil or baby oil in your palm, rub hands until they're well covered, then sprinkle on 1 teaspoon of sugar and do the same. Rinse them off under warm water.

- Want to get all the lotion out of the bottle? Put it in the microwave briefly — but be sure to remove the top if it's metal. It will become thin enough to pour, but will thicken to the usual consistency when it's cool.

If You're Allergic to Costume Jewelry …

- I have friends whose skin breaks out if they wear anything other than surgical steel, gold or sterling silver. (It seems to me this is a great rumor to start about yourself). However, at least one of them confided to me that she has figured out a system for wearing costume jewelry. She applies moleskin (a padding from the foot-care department) to the clip part of earrings or to the skin side of pierced earrings that come with gold or silver posts. The moleskin works inside a bracelet, too.

Testing ...
Testing ...

In The Kitchen

Is the dish microwavable?

Put a glass measuring cup filled with 1/2 cup water into the microwave oven and put the dish for testing near but not touching it. Microwave on high for one minute. If the water is hot but the dish is not...it's microwavable. If the dish is hot (or even has hot spots), it is not. Don't use this test on dishes with metal trim — they aren't microwavable.

What's the wattage of the oven?

• Make a pitcher of well-iced water and strain a cup into a glass measuring cup. Place in the center of a cool microwave oven that hasn't been used overnight. Turn it on to 100 percent power. If the water boils in 3-1/2 minutes or less, it's a high-wattage oven (about 750-800 watts). If it takes five minutes, it is a low-wattage oven. (about 500-600 watts).

Is the yeast good?

• Stir your yeast and 1 tablespoon sugar in the amount of warm water called for. Let it sit for 10 minutes. If it foams, it is good.

Has the canned milk turned?

• Pour some into a small amount of coffee. If it's sour, it will curdle immediately.

Has the baking soda deteriorated?

• Test for freshness by adding 1/4 teaspoon of baking soda to a tablespoon of vinegar. If the baking soda bubbles, it's still good.

Has the mold spoiled everything?

• Cut away small spots on hard cheese, salami, firm fruits and vegetables (leaving an inch clearance around the spot). Rewrap and place in clean container. Spoon away spots on jam (leaving an inch clearance). Discard all other dairy and baked products, dried peas and beans, flour, nuts, corn on the cob and peanut butter.

Around The House

Is this the front door key?

- Have the hole in the house key drilled a little off-center and it will be easy to distinguish from the rest on your ring.

Is the toilet-tank valve leaking?

- Pour some bluing into the tank. Don't flush for an hour or more. If blue water appears in the bowl, replace the valve.

Where's the gas leak coming from?

- Make a solution of soapy water with dishwasher detergent. Use a brush to lather the gas pipes. Escaping gas will cause the soapy water to bubble, revealing the damaged areas. Make a temporary plug by moistening a cake of soap and pressing it over the spot to close the leak until the gas man comes. But that's only a temporary and not completely effective remedy. You must call the gas man IMMEDIATELY.

Which circuit breaker to flip?

- Plug in a portable radio in the room where you want to turn off the power, turning it up loud enough to hear at the fuse box. When you flip the right switch, the radio will shut off.

Are the car headlights properly aligned?

- Park on a flat surface three to four feet from wall or garage door. Turn on low beam and mark a circle of light on the wall or door. Back up 35 feet, leaving your low beams on. The circle from this distance should be no higher than your original marks.

Where's the slow leak?

- Mark a starting point and slowly revolve the tire, moving a "studfinder" across the tread until you find the small nail or tack. This works on steel-treaded tires, too.

Has the power been interrupted?

- When you're going on vacation, or when you leave a weekend house, leave a coin or bottlecap on top of one of the ice cube tray sections; or leave some cubes in a bowl. If the coin is in the middle of the cube, or if the bowl contains one solid piece of ice, the power has gone off.

Is the (cartridge-type) fuse good?

- Use a flashlight, and substitute the fuse for one of the batteries. If the flashlight lights, the fuse is okay.

Does the battery have any life left?

- Use just a tiny (jellybean-sized) bulb and a pair of pliers. Place the battery's negative end on one handle of a pair of pliers. Hold the bulb's base to the battery's positive end and touch the base with the other plier handle to complete the circuit. If the bulb lights, then the battery has some life in it.

Is there a water leak that isn't showing?

- Use a flashlight again. Press the end of the flashlight (not the rubber type) onto an exposed water line and put your ear to the light part. If there is a leak, you will hear a faint ticking sound.

Is the paint on the walls latex or oil-based?

- Get Goof-Off from the hardware store and apply a tiny bit to a hidden area, then scrub. If the paint gums up, it's latex. If what you've done just makes the area slightly cleaner, the paint is oil-based.

Buying A House?

Is the roofing slate in good condition?

- Knock on it. If it sounds like wood or cardboard, it's dead. It should have a ring, like a heavy sheet of plate glass.

How old are the bathroom fixtures?

- Look inside the toilet tank and you'll find the year of manufacture. Unless the toilet has been replaced, you'll get a pretty good idea of when the bathroom — and probably the house itself — was built.

In The Laundry

Will the fabric bleed?

- Wash with a scrap of white fabric. If it runs, either wash it separately or set the colors by soaking them for half an hour in a gallon of cold water to which you've added 1/2 cup salt. Then wash in cool water.

Is the powdered detergent stale?

- Shake the box. If you can hear the powder move, the detergent is in good condition. If the powder is old and caked together, it won't do as efficient a job.

Is your water hard or soft?

- Put a teaspoon of soap flakes in a jar with 2 cups of warm water, cover and shake. If you get a lot of suds and they last up to five minutes, the water is soft. If only a few suds appear and they last only a short time, the water is hard.

Is the item colorfast?

- Make sudsy water at the temperature of your wash water and soak a corner of the item in the suds for a few minutes. If the water has become colored — the item will run. Or simply rub an inside seam with a wet cloth to see if the color rubs off.

When You're Shopping

Is the fabric synthetic?

- Burn a small strip or a few threads. If the results are a fine ash that powders when you rub it between your thumb and forefinger, it's made of natural fiber (cotton, silk, wool, linen or a blend of same). An ash that leaves a glass bead-type residue comes from a synthetic. This is a test that works both for fabric and for rugs.

What size rug to order?

- Cut and paste sections of newspaper together to try out various sizes on the floor. Then make your selection.

How much fabric to buy?

- Fold a sheet to the same width as the fabric you plan on using. Lay the pattern pieces out on it and measure.

Is the hardware (or bed) solid brass or just brass-plated?

- Take a magnet with you. If the item is steel underneath, the magnet will cling to it.

For The Gardener

Is the fertilizer correct?

- Check the nitrogen content rather than price. Higher levels of nitrogen encourage lush green growth at the expense of flowers and fruit.

Is the soil draining properly?

- Don't plant a tree in soil that has poor drainage. Check by filling the hole with water. If it hasn't drained in twelve hours, your tree won't do well.

Are the seeds still good?

- Count out about fifty, placing them between two layers of wet newspaper covered with a plate. After five days, count the number of seeds that have germinated to determine how thickly they will have to be spread. If half are no longer good, use twice as many as you normally would.

Bed and Bath

Is the sheet on straight?

- You can embroider or mark small designs on the sheet to indicate where it should line up with the lower corner of the bed. Easier still, when you fold your sheets, make the first fold vertical and use the crease line as a guide in bedmaking.

Which moisturizer to choose?

- Dab on a drop or two. Moisturizer that's good for oily skin should evaporate quickly and leave your skin feeling cool. Dry skin moisturizer should feel warm, because it should stay on the skin's surface.

Is your calcium supplement effective?

- Some calcium supplements don't seem to be absorbed properly. Test yours by dropping a tablet into a glass of vinegar. It should dissolve within 30 minutes.

---

*I don't think it's fair that in order to clean anything ...
you have to get something else dirty!*

Are you allergic to your bath soak?

• Some people like to make their own bath soak by selecting a group of herbs—such as dried lavender flowers, rosemary, thyme, and dried mint; or camomile and rose petals—and tying them into doubled thicknesses of cheesecloth to make sachets. Put sachets into the tub, pour very hot water over them, and let them steep for ten minutes. If you may be allergic, you may want to try a spot test by applying a dot of the product or herb the size of a matchhead (if the mixture isn't liquid, add to it a drop or two of mineral oil) on a ½ inch piece of unmedicated gauze. Place patch on a hair-free area of skin on inside of arm or back and leave for 48 hours without getting wet. If it burns, itches, aches or even feels irritable, remove patch and flush area with water. If there is redness, swelling pimples, blisters or itching within 2 to 48 hours, you're probably allergic.

Is your hair healthy?

• Cut off one strand, wet it thoroughly and stretch it. Healthy hair stretches about 1/3 again the length of the original without breaking, then springs back when released. Damaged hair breaks before stretching that far and/or stays stretched.

Are you well-balanced?

• A pilot's medical exam requires that you do the following with eyes closed: stand with feet together without swaying for 10 seconds, and hold your arms straight out at shoulder height and touch your toes with alternating hands.

The Littlest Room

Hair Treatments

- Want a quick pickup for hairs left on a bathmat? Slip on a pair of rubber gloves and run your hand across it. Hair draws toward it like a magnet without sticking to the gloves
- And to get hairs out of the sink drain, insert a long, slender fondu fork and twist. Yucckky — but cheaper than a plumber. (Next time, put a bit of netting down deep in the drain and it will catch those hairs. Replace it from time to time.)

Temperature Control

- Mark the chrome bathtub handles and the tile above them with red dots (buy them at the stationery store; they're used for marking file folders). Place them so that when the two are in alignment, the bath temperature is just right. This is a safety measure, too.

To Prevent Soap Slipping out of Your Hand

- Put the bar into a stocking, tie a knot, and tie the end to your faucet or the shower bar.
- Make homemade soap on a rope: Select your favorite brand, drill a hole with a 5/16" bit about an inch from the end. (Use decorative cord and you've made a nice gift.)

Quick Fixes

- **Shower Curtain** – If the plastic shower curtain is torn where hooks are attached, reinforce the spot with a cornpad (the kind that has a hole in it) inside the curtain and outside the liner; or make a new hole with a paper punch, and protect it with grommets from the fabric store.
- **Sink Stopper** – When the metal stopper in the sink won't come up, don't use a sharp tool, since it might nick the edge and damage the stopper. A small suction cup will do the trick.

I believe that the best motivation for housecleaning is having a party.

Four Items that Cut Your Bathroom Cleaning in Half

- **A Sponge.** (White nylon scouring sponge if you've got hard water, or a a cellulose sponge if you've got soft water.) Get the family to sponge the ring around the tub when they get up and before they step out of the tub.

- **Bubble Bath.** Not only does it feel nice, it eliminates ring around the tub. Experiment until you find one that works; kids' hair shampoo works fine for me.

- **Squeegee.** Hang it near the shower. Ask family to use it after each use. You won't have a problem with mildew and accumulated deposits.

- **Furniture Wax.** Wax and buff the basins and shower walls. (Not tub bottom; it'll be too slippery.) Soap film won't accumulate, and lime and minerals will be repelled. You'll clean much less often.

Scales Before Your Eyes

- Want your bathroom scale to be accurate? Set two five-pound bags of sugar on scales, one bag in the spot where each of your feet would be, and turn the dial until it says 10 pounds. Lift the bags and set them down again, until the 10-pound mark stays steady. Then the scale will be in balance. (Personally, I prefer to greet the morning on a scale that registers a little underweight.)

Soap Dish Timesavers

- Spray non-stick vegetable oil on the dish to make it easier to clean.
- Wrap the dish with plastic wrap and discard that periodically.
- Leave a piece of sponge under the soap.
- Or, use liquid soap.

Curling Iron

- Remove hair spray from a COOL curling iron with fingernail polish remover.
- Or rub it with an emery board.

To Hold Supplies

- Great holder for bathroom soaps, toys, bottles: A triple set of hanging wire-mesh kitchen baskets.

Toilet

- Remove mineral stains from toilets. Pour in chlorine bleach, swish with brush, flush. If stains persist, empty bowl by pouring a bucket of water into the tank. Now add vinegar and rub stains with a scrubbing pad. Or try this labor-saver: drop half a swimming pool chlorine tablet in the tank.

Soap Bars

What I do when I have a little piece of soap left is just dampen it and stick it onto the new bar. If you want something a little fancier, here are two ways to make new bars from old soap:
- "Patchwork bars": Put five or six slivers in a one-quart glass bowl with 1/4 cup water. Microwave on high for 45-60 seconds, drain water, slide slivers onto a square of aluminum foil, push into a bar shape and fold foil around them, molding soap as you do Let the soap bar stand until it's hard, then peel off foil.
- Glycerine soap: Add a jarful of boiling water to half a jar of scraps. Add juice of a lemon and a teaspoon of glycerine, mix well and shape. When cool, the soap will wash hands and keep them soft.

Liquid Soap

You can make your own liquid soap from soap scraps.
- Cut it with a knife until it's the size of cornmeal, put scraps in a jar, add hot water and shake.
- Shred bits from the kind of soap that has moisture cream (about the equivalent of a 3.5 oz bar), add 3 cups of water and microwave at high setting 5-6 minutes, stirring every 2 minutes. Let stand until cool. Mixture will thicken slightly.

Non-Slip Strips

- To clean them, scrub with a solution of one-half cup turpentine and two tablespoons of detergent.

Blowdryer Holder

- I found the perfect spot to park my blow dryer: the bathroom glass holder. The hole fits most nozzles perfectly

Where to Keep Your Towels?

RACK THEM... Look for hotel-style towel racks that consist of several metal rings sticking out horizontally from the mounting. The ones I use hold four each of washclothes, hand towels, and bathtowels right on the bathroom wall. Or roll them so they'll fit a wall-mounted wine rack.

PEG THEM... Replace towel bars with pegs and you'll be able to hang several towels where you had only one.

ROLL THEM... A supply of washclothes can be rolled and kept in a small basket, a collection of larger ones left in a picnic basket on the floor.

...OR SACK THEM. Give family members terry robes to use instead of bathtowels. New double-sided hooks slip over shower curtain rod and hold robes.

Cabinet Organizers

- Put a small magnetic bar inside the cabinet to hold clippers, tweezers, scissors and file.
- Coat cans of shaving cream, hair spray, etc. with clear nail polish so you don't leave a rust ring inside the medicine cabinet.

Curtain Time

- Before you hang a new shower curtain or liner, cover the top part of the shower with clear weather stripping tape, then repunch the holes so they'll be reinforced.
- To keep the curtain to the shower wall, put a strip of velcro on each.
- Spray WD-40 along the rod and you'll be less likely to get tears.
- Hang a second curtain liner in front of the shower wall to protect it from soap scum and mineral deposits. It's easier to toss the liner in the machine with a couple of towels than it is to scrub the wall.

Mold Deterrent

- Trim the bottom of the shower curtain liner with pinking shears and mildew is less likely to accumulate.
- If mildew has already grown along the hem, just cut it off, and add a second row of rings at the top. Even though it's slightly shorter at the top as a result, the curtain will offer you enough protection.

Track Lightening

- A disposable sponge paintbrush with a tapered end makes a great tool for cleaning the shower track.
- But if the shower track is really dirty, the best solution is to remove the doors so you can clean it thoroughly. Hold it with one hand on each side while lifting it off the track. You may need a helper.

A bad case of planning: spring fever and spring cleaning arrive at the same time.

What's Got You Floored?

Cement

Mold?

- Wash with a solution of chlorine bleach.

Graffiti?

- Use Mex Multi-Purpose Cleaner (from the hardware store). Or, with extreme caution, mix a cup of lye with a gallon of water in a plastic pail. Wear rubber gloves. Brush solution onto graffiti with an old broom. Rinse thoroughly.

Metal stains?

- Use a solution of oxalic acid powder and water.

Rust?

- Sprinkle Portland Cement on stain, then sprinkle on water and work cement into stain with a brisk push broom. Rinse off. (Use this for oil stains, too).
- For tough cases, mix ten parts water and one part of muriatic acid; or slowly add a pound of oxalic acid to a gallon of water. (Caution: splashing is dangerous; wear goggles, rubber gloves and boots). Apply with an old mop (discard it afterwards), let set 2-3 hours, then rinse with a stiff-bristled, non-metallic brush. (Use extreme caution)
- Or hire a professional pressure cleaner service.

Hardwood

(ALWAYS TRY ANY SOLUTION ON A WOOD FLOOR IN AN INCONSPICUOUS SPOT BEFORE APPLYING IT TO THE WHOLE AREA, JUST IN CASE THERE IS STAINING OR LIGHTENING).

Staple marks? Or other marks?

- Sand area, save the sand and mix it with white glue to make a paste. Fill holes, let dry overnight, resand. Stain area to match surrounding wood.
- Or fill with paste wax, then buff.
- Or drill a hole slightly larger than the problem, fill with colored wood putty or wax stick, sand and wax.

Dirty?

- Use turpentine or white vinegar.

Scuff marks?

- Try Crisco.

Need coverups?

- Paste shoe polish in a matching color will stain and shine.
- To match a wood stain, mix oil paints to match. Paint on, wax, and buff. (Best colors to start with are these three: yellow ochre, burnt sienna and white).

Squeaks?

- Sprinkle talcum powder over the cracks and rub it in.

No-Wax

Sticky?

- Use Murphy's Oil Soap (1/4 cup to one gallon warm water). Apply it with a sponge, then rinse the area with clear, warm water.

Yellowing?

- After cleaning, mix 1/4 cup Spic and Span and 1 cup ammonia in 1/2 gallon of water. Apply to one 3-foot square area at a time. Let soak five minutes, rinse with clear water on a sponge.

Dull?

- To replace gloss after stripping with ammonia, use applications of wax. Allow each coat to dry thoroughly between applications.

Linoleum

Need coverups?

- Automobile touchup paint. Will cover scratches and burns. It's hard to clean off, so work with a fine-haired brush for careful application.
- Sand a burn mark with fine sandpaper, rinse with 1 cup vinegar in a quart of water, then apply acrylic paint mixed to match with a small brush. After 15-20 minutes, seal with acrylic varnish.

Dented areas?

- Put a piece of fabric or brown garbage bag (several layers) over the spot, then iron over that. Put a gallon jug filled with very hot water on each spot for half an hour, remove, and re-iron spots.

Scuff marks?

- Fine steel wool.
- Wipe with a small amount of kerosene or turpentine. Don't cover a large area with either of these as they are very flammable.
- Try an ordinary pencil eraser.
- Or rub on Crisco.
- Or baking soda.
- Or WD-40.

Slate

Dull?

- Clean, dry fireplace hearth slate can be made lustrous with lemon oil. Wipe to remove excess.
- Soap-type cleaners will leave scum on slate, which is porous. Use washing soda or a synthetic detergent; or try Spic and Span monthly along with an alcohol and water rinse.
- Or clean with Dawn dish soap in hot water, then rinse with lemon juice in water to remove soapy residue; clean afterward regularly with lemon juice in warm water. Full-strength Dawn can set briefly on stubborn spots but remove residue afterwards.
- Or use one part boric acid to two parts water. Wash from top to bottom with thick sponge (don't go back and forth) and air- or fan- dry.
- Or protect slate with a cement sealer and then use a self-polishing wax. Futura is good.
- Paint remover takes old wax and dirt off real slate floors.

Tile

Damaged area of resiliant flooring?

- Take a scrap piece larger than the damaged spot, and tape it on top. Cut through both layers at the same time, and you'll have a perfectly sized, tight-fitting patch.

Loose tiles?

- With electric iron on a low setting, iron the tile to melt the adhesive. Lift tile, then spread new glue and reapply.
- Or inject some sealer in a hypodermic needle. Lay down boards covered with heavy books or other weights until glue is dry.
- Or peel the tile up when the heat softens the glue, coat bare patches on tile bottom with a vinyl adhesive and lay the tile again. Use weights as above.

Vacuuming

- The biggest help in getting regular vacuuming done is to have the vacuum someplace where it's easy to get to. (The more often you vacuum, the less often your rug needs a real deep cleaning. Get one vacuum for upstairs and one for down, if possible.

- Add a thirty-foot extension cord to the vacuum so you can drag it from room to room without replugging — but be sure to tie the end of the vacuum cord and extension cord together in a simple knot. That way, if you give the machine a yank, you won't pull the cord out of the wall.

- Put some dried beans in the disposable bag. When air makes the beans move, they compact the dust and you change the bag less frequently.

- I love Bissell's Deep Cleaning Machine. It gives the same type of wet deep cleaning action as professional-style carpet cleaning services provide. Nothing is better for keeping your carpet fresh and stain free. It's also wonderful for cleaning upholstery, mattresses, stuffed animals, floors — a bunch of things.

I would like to go down in history as the inventor of the dish that washes itself, then returns to the cupboard.

When You've Got It Together

Here's Where to Put It

"What do women really want?" Freud asked. I could have told him:
More storage. Here are new ways to find storage space ...
and better ways to store what you've got.

Bedroom Storage: Linens and Out-of-Season Clothing

- You can have night tables and extra storage all in one. Buy 40-gallon garbage pails, either plastic or metal, have a round plywood top made, and cover with a circular cloth that hangs to the floor. For an extra touch, have a glass cover made as well.
- Or make a night table out of a clothes hamper.
- Or fasten casters to an old dresser drawer (or two) and slide them under the bed. You've got extra storage that's easy to roll in and out.

Blankets and Quilts

- If you don't have room to stow those extra blankets in your closets (or in luggage), tuck them between the mattress and the box spring.
- If you haven't room (or money) for one of those elegant quilt hangers at the end of your bed, put up a curtain rod inside the bedroom door to hang the quilt.

Brooms and Mops

- You don't need elaborate gadgets to keep the broom and mop off the floor. It's easy to insert an inexpensive little cup hook into the handle, then just hang the item from a nail.

Coins

- A plastic medicine bottle can hold coins for the laundromat or the toll machines on the highway. Three inches holds $8 worth of quarters.

Coupons and Recipes

- Glue a cork board inside the kitchen cabinet doors and the coupons and recipes will be nearby but not cluttering up the room.

Dry Goods

- Sugar and flour will stay bug-free, dry and easy to measure if you use a funnel to pour them right out of the bag into a clean, dry clear plastic milk carton or soda bottle.

Kitchenware

- Solve a seating and storage problem all in one. Make your breakfast table base by screwing together two or three kitchen cabinets (30" high wall cabinets work well), then have a formica top made to order.
- That awkward cupboard on top of the refrigerator may serve you better if you take off the doors and install vertical dividers. Now you've got a place for your cutting boards, trays, cookie sheets and cake racks.
- A pretty plastic flower pot catches drips, holds lots of kitchen implements.

Holiday Supplies

- Wrap ornaments in egg cartons, bulb cartons, or liquor cartons.
- Save wrapping paper in garment bag or long florist's boxes; or slip the paper inside the cardboard roll to prevent it from getting dog-eared.
- Ribbons can be rolled around the cardboard roll in a plastic wrap or foil dispenser.

Night-Table Items

• If you haven't room on your night table for your glasses, a note pad, pack of tissues, etc., take two placemats, cut one in half and sew it to the front of the other to create a pocket. The extra length can be tucked between the mattress and box spring.

Photographs

• I don't like to put every nice photo into the album. If I did, we'd have more albums than anyone would care to look through. Yet I hate to throw the extras away. I store them efficiently in a 4x6 card file. It's a great place to store the negatives, too. Use card separators to indicate what month and year the photos were taken. Dip into this file to send a photo with a letter or by itself, as a picture postcard (a laundry marker writes on the reverse surface most easily). And looking through the files is almost as easy as glancing through an album.

Phone Numbers

• Who says you need to have an address book?. File your friends names and addresses on 3x5 cards. If there's a change, you can simply make a new card. On the card, there's also lots of room to jot down other information - such as birthdates, etc. File cards for service people (P for Plumber), Society Security and other numbers (file under S), credit card numbers (under C), insurance policies (under I) — or in whatever way you'd look them up.

• Alternatively, I saw one of those six-sided "photo cubes" used for phone numbers instead of photos. Much faster than looking up numbers in a book; each side can hold a portion of the alphabet.

Plastic Bags

- An empty tissue box is a fine place for storing extra bags from the grocery for recycling. If you've got the time, you can fold them into each other (check out how they do it in the box of tissues) so they'll pop up. Or just jam them in.
- Or take an odd sock and cut off the ribbing. Use it like a napkin ring to hold bags.
- Or push bags down one end of an empty cardboard tube, and when you need one, pull it out the other end.
- Or shove them down the neck of an empty plastic gallon jug and make a small hole in the bottom of the jug to pull them out.

Rubber Gloves

- They'll be really handy but neatly out of sight if you put up a spring clothespin inside your kitchen cabinet door to hold them.

Stuffed Toys

- Put up a wooden dowel that reaches from floor to ceiling. Or check in the carpet store to see if you can get the sturdy center roll from a length of carpeting. Sew ribbons on the toys and dolls, and put hooks on the dowel or roll.

Bath Toys

- Store bath toys in a mesh lingerie bag. Tie with a string and hang it over the showerhead so the toys drip-dry.

Ideas for Hang-Ups

- Storage shelves can be hung easily with lengths of link chains and eight S hooks: four fastened to shelf corners and four fastened to the ceiling or beam above. Easy to remove, relocate, adjust.
- Wooden dowels, painted or stained as you prefer, fastened with cafe curtain hooks, can make a towel rack in small nooks or behind cabinet doors in kitchen or bath.
- Metal utility towel racks can be used to store poles, rods, pipes, lengths of narrow lumber, etc. if you attach a pair of them vertically to studs in basement or garage and rest the items in between.

Toilet Paper

- Place a boutique-size tissue box cover over a roll of good quality toilet paper, thread the end of the roll through the slot on top, and you have an attractive, long lasting and less expensive bathroom tissue.

Sewing Supplies

- A garment bag, the kind used for storing sweaters is ideal for keeping fabric and sewing notions neat and tidy.

Sports Equipment

- Paint a gym locker to match the decor of your teenage son's room. It'll hold mitts, bats, helmets, skateboards, hockey sticks. You name it! Plus it looks good too.

Tableclothes

- Store them rolled over cardboard rolls and they'll be crease- and wrinkle-free. (And if they're wrong side out, they won't get dust lines or yellow marks).

Table Pads

- Often it is possible to stow them right under the table. Find the right kind of hook or angle iron and install them so pads can rest under them.

Twist Ties

- You can use a toothpick holder to hold all those extra ties that come in the box of plastic bags. Or put them in the empty tin box that held the bandage strips.

Clothes Conscious

- To hold belts, remove a large (2- or 3-inch) ring from a three-ring binder, and hang it horizontally in your closet. You can flip the belts to the top of the ring until the one you want is in the right position to be removed.

- Jewelry box a mess? Line a large, shallow drawer with a light color, textured carpet remnant. Beads, chains, broaches, earrings, even rings stay put. Neat storage...and easy selection at a glance.

- To maximize closet space, take the plastic ring off a milk jug and place it over the top of a hanger, then hang another hanger from it. I can hang two or three blouses in the space of one.

- That old TV cart can be used in a closet to hold your shoes and bags. The height is convenient and you can roll out the cart for easy cleaning.

- Store kids' pants on multiple skirt hangers. Also, use a dowel, hung with chains from the regular rod, to make a second, lower rod. You'll be able to get twice as much in the same space.

- Use a shoe bag to hold winter accessories. Or put up spring-type clothespins.

Office Surprise

Check out the office supply store for items that can help you get organized at home. For example:

- Storage files: Use inexpensive, quickly assembled files to organize school and household papers and and get them out of the way. Cover the front with spray paint or contact paper if you want a decorator touch.

- Vertical files, meant to separate papers and hold file folders, can keep your home file folders straight, but also do duty in the kitchen: organize trays and cookie sheets, large plastic lids, plastic place mats...and more.
- Pocket files and clipboards can be mounted on a kitchen wall, used to keep PTA memos, bills, etc. handy.

Greatest Storage Helper of All Time: Liquor Cartons

The boxes are sturdy and come with a variety of different dividers. The four-section ones that hold jug wine, for instance, are big enough to store shoes or, during a move, to hold lamp bases. Twelve-section ones are great for kitchen utensils and glassware, mittens, caps and scarves. Minibottle cartons can hold makeup and medicine cabinet items, Christmas ornaments and zillions of other items. They're invaluable when you move because you can get at your cosmetics and kitchen supplies before you're settled in and without having to unpack the whole box.

I Store These Things in the Refrigerator

- Nail polish won't get gummy if stored in the refrig.
- Plastic wrap. I used to hate using the stuff. It never stuck to anything but itself. But when I store it in the refrigerator it really does work better.
- Keep your candles cold and they'll burn slower, so they last longer.
- Angora sweaters shed all over the place. You can stop some of the shedding by storing the sweater in the freezer a few hours before wearing.

I won't worry about "getting it all together" until I figure out where I'll put it.

Did You Know?

How to Preserve a Newspaper Clipping?

- Dissolve a milk of magnesia tablet in a quart of club soda overnight. Pour into a pan large enough to accommodate the flattened newspaper. Soak clipping for an hour, remove and pat dry. Estimated life: 200 years.

How to Track Down a Product or Manufacturer?

- I get so many letters from people trying unsuccessfully to find a particular brand that a local store no longer stocks or to locate the manufacturer of their appliance to find out about replacement parts. The best way to do this is through your local library. There are reference books that list holders of trademarks and company names and addresses.

How to Treat the Sponge So It Won't Stick to the Frost-Free Freezer?

- Sprinkle it with windshield washer cleaner.

How to Check the Mailbox without Going Outdoors?

- Paint a #2 can lid a bright color and tie it to a piece of nylon cord. Fasten the cord's other end to a bracket above the mailbox and wedge the can lid inside the rim of the box. When the lid is dangling, you know the postman has brought you something.

How to Get the Childproof Lid Off?

- Take a pliers and remove the top. That exposes the perfectly fine screw-on type lid underneath.

How to Get a Signed I.O.U. When You Have None?

• If you have lent someone a large amount of money and have no IOU — here's what to do. Send a letter to the person mentioning the loan, but describe it as twice the amount. You'll probably get back a letter stating that you only lent half that much. The letter will be your proof if you have to collect on the loan!

How to Water a Hanging Houseplant Without the Drips?

• Hang an umbrella with a handle from the edge of the plant (upside down) and it will catch all the drips.

Faking It

In order to be a good wife you have to learn to fake a lot of things. Right girls? Here are a few of my favorites:

• Faking cleaning: Add a ¼ cup of pine scented cleaner to a spray bottle and fill with water. Before a snoopy neighbor walks in the door, spritz the place down and she'll think you've been scrubbing all day. Or rearrange the furniture.

• Faking gardening: When your violets are in a slump, just add artificial blossoms to the sick plant and it will look good as new!

• Faking cooking: Saute an onion in a little oil. Everyone will smell the "home cooking" and you can serve a take out meal without anybody knowing.

Share your favorite original hints with us. If we use them we will send you a copy of one of my books.

Send to: Mary Ellen
            P.O. Box 39221
            Edina, MN 55439

Happy hinting!

WOW! Mary Ellen's Products Really Work

MARY ELLEN'S WOW! FORMULA 1 AND FORMULA 2:

"As every homemaker knows, seeing spots isn't a medical problem. It's an occupational hazard."

You won't be seeing spots for long if you use these miracle stain removers. Just squirt on and stains disappear without rubbing or scrubbing. Before your eyes: wine, coffee, tea, fruit drinks, gravy, lipstick, collar rings, perspiration and many more. Formula 1 is for whites and bleachable colors; Formula 2 is for colored clothes.

BYE BYE BABY STAINS

"After the miracle of childbirth comes the miracle of laundry."

How does one little baby generate such a mess? So many moms asked me for a way to remove formula, spit-ups and other baby stains that we decided there was a need for this one-of-a-kind product. Squirt it on and watch most impossible stains disappear ... even old stains from hand-me-downs will be "all gone."

FOR THOSE DAYS

"To me PMS comes after the fact. To me it means 'Pretty Messy Stuff'."

Ladies, I ask you, is there anything more annoying than all those pretty underthings that have been ruined by menstrual stains? A set-in blood stain was impossible to remove until now. FOR THOSE DAYS removes those stains in seconds. I guarantee it!

BLEACH BOOSTER

"I believe the best thing you can do in the laundry room is leave it."

But when you use BLEACH BOOSTER at least you'll leave with the brightest and whitest clothes on the block. A couple of squirts to a cup of liquid bleach will increase it's power by 200%. You talk about clothing, bedding, uniforms and towels being white. You'll have to wear shades.

BATHROOM STAINS DOWN THE DRAIN

"The good news about cleaning the bathroom is that at least it's the smallest room in the house."

No matter how big or small your bathroom is, you'll love this for removing tough bathroom stains: mineral deposits, water marks, soap and oil, embedded dirt and soap build-up. It's easy to use too.

Look for my unique WOW! Stain Removers in your favorite supermarket, fabric center, or mass merchandiser. If you have any trouble locating them or would like more information, call toll free 1-800-328-6294.

Don't Say Oops — Say Mary Ellen's WOW!

How to Order More Books

If you'd like to order more copies of this book for graduations, birthdays, holidays or any other gift occasion, here's how:

1-5 books	$6.95 per book
5-10 books	$6.25 per book
10-20 books	$5.25 per book
20-40 books	$4.50 per book
40-up books	$3.48 per book

All prices include postage and handling.
Minnesota residents add 6½% sales tax.

Send a check or money order to Mary Ellen, P.O. Box 39221, Edina, MN 55439. FOR ORDERS OVER $20.00 CALL TOLL FREE 1-800-328-6294.

I've got other books too. Send for a free catalog: Mary Ellen Catalog, P.O. Box 39221, Edina, MN 55439

Index

Bird: *repelling, building nests, 94; capturing when escaped, 99*
Bird seed: *99*
Birdcage: *catching birdseed, 99*
Birthdays: *infants' parties, 82; special decorations, 82*
Blankets: *storing, 16; 19; 131*
Bleach: *cleaning vegetables, 33; dangers of, 54*
Blender: *hand-held mixer instead of, 72;*
Blinds: *See* Venetian blinds
Blowdryer: *holder, 122*
Boiling: *pot boiling over, 73; water boiling away, 73*
Books: *musty, 21*
Borax: *uses, 35,76; preserving flowers, 50*
Boots: *to keep mud off, 35*
Bowl covers: *improvised, 32*
Box Elder bugs: *repelling, 94*
Braces: *cleaning, 105; when picture taking, 105*
Brass: *testing for solid, 115*
Breakfast table: *inexpensive custom made, 132*
Bric A Brac: *repairing, 21*
Brick: *cleaning, 125*
Broken glass: *cleaning up, 24*
Brooms: *storing, 131*
Brown sugar: *softening, 18*
Brushes: *cleaning, 35, 40*
Bubble bath: *homemade, 56; preventing tub ring, 120*
Bug spray: *homemade, 96*
Bugs: *See* Insect control
Bulletin board: *for children, 85; in laundry room, 78*
Bumps: *swelling, 87*
Burns: *cover-up, 52*
Butcher block: *cleaning, 62*
Buttons: *securing, 42*
Cabinets: *organizers, 122*
Cakes: *icing, 32; lumpy,67*
Calcium supplement: *testing whether effective, 116*
Calculator: *stuck buttons, 35*
Can opener: *cutting wheel "frozen", 21*

Candles: *slow burning, 137*
Candy: *freezing for children, 86; hardened, 24-25*
Canned milk: *freshness test, 111*
Caps: *hanging up, 19*
Car doors: *stuck, 35*
Car locks: *frozen, 35*
Cards, Christmas: *uses for, 16*
Cards, get well: *addressing, 18*
Cards, greeting: *uses for, 16*
Carpet: *cleaning, 34; cleaning indoor/outdoor, 63; deodorizing, 35; flat pile, 21; spills, 15; what size to buy, 115; wine stain, 35*
Cats: *controlling, 95; dry bathing, 100; feeding, 100; grooming, 102; See also* Pets
Cat litter: *as deodorizer, 15*
Cedar: *renewing scent in, 22*
Ceiling: *removing stains, 22*
Cement: *cleaning, 125*
Chandelier: *cleaner, 55*
Chewing gum: *in hair, 17*
Child care tips: *81-87*
Child-proof lids: *removing, 139*
Children: *bulletin board for, 85; bumps and scrapes, 87; closet tips, 83; clothing, reinforcing of, 83-84; discipline, 85-87; dressing tips, 82; enforcing "taking turns", 85; face-cleaning, 82; getting dressed faster, 85; getting home on time, 85; illness, 87; interrupting phone calls, 85; learning left/right shoes, 85; learning to button, 86; making clay for, 53; making finger paint for, 52; point system for rules, 85; schoolwork storage, 19; See also* Babies; *serving drinks to, 17, 86; shoe tying, 86; shoe untying,86; using cup (in bath), 86; warming kids' bed, 30; water play to soothe, 85*
China: *coffee stains, 34*
Chlorine products: *dangers of, 54*
Chopping: *with small food processor, 72*

Ice cream: *crystalling, 71*
Ice cream muffins: *49*

Ice cube tray: *to store beads and sequins, 37*
Iced tea: *cloudy, 68; storing of, 68*
ID tags: *from credit cards, 34*
Insects: *in closet, 33; on house plants, 96*
Insect control: *93-97; in stored food, 18, 132*
Insect spray: *homemade, 96*
Instant ice pack: *how to make, 34*
Ironing: *neat clothes without, 75; preparing garment, 19*
I.O.U.: *getting one signed, 140*
Jar lid: *stuck, 71*
Jeans: *smooth without ironing, 75; stone-washing of, 77*
Jewelry: *cleaning, 57; storing, 19, 136*
Kahlua liqueur: *homemade, 58*
Keys: *finding door key on ring, 112*
Kitchen appliances: *See* appliances
Kitchen shears: *uses for, 72*
Kitchen: *inexpensive table, 132; storing dry goods, 132; storing rubber gloves, 134; uses for plastic flower pot, 132; using over fridge cupboard, 132*
Knitting: *storing, 40, 42*
Knives: *rusty, 24*
Kool-aid : *on children's faces, 82*
Lasagna: *48*
Laundry: *75-79; 114-115*
Laundry: *spot cleaning, 43; too "stiff", 78*
Leaks: *gas, 112; water, 113*
Leaves: *preserving, 50*
Leftovers: *beverages for ice cubes, 18*
Leg warmers: *making for children, 83*
Lemon scented spray: *homemade, 53*
Letter writing: *amusing enclosures, 19*
Linen: *storing, 131*

Linoleum: *burns and scratches, 127; cover-ups (matching), 127; dented, 127; leftovers as shelf liner, 17; scuffed, 127*
Lint: *on furniture, 16*
Lip gloss: *improvised, 106*
Liquers: *homemade, 58*
Liquid soap: *uses, 34; homemade, 122*
Liquor cartons: *for storage, 137*
Litter boxes: *deodorizing, 102; inexpensive liners, 102*
Logs for fireplace: *from newspapers, 59*
Loofah: *slimy, 26*
Lost and found: *on home, 85*
Lotion: *using all in bottle, 109*
Luggage: *keeping fresh, 16*
Macrame: *cleaning, 61*
Magnetic knife rack: *uses, 32*
Mail orders: *keeping track, 18*
Mailbox: *checking for mail, 139*
Manufacturer: *locating, 139*
Marble floor: *cleaning, 63*
Marshmallows: *hardened, 24*
Mashed potatoes: *not smooth, 68*
Measuring cup: *from ice cream scoop, 29*
Meat: *cubing, 72; "fully cooked" test, 111*
Meatballs: *shaping, 67*
Meatloaf: *cracking, 67*
Medical diary: *for children, 87*
Medicine: *bad tasting, 87*
Mending pants: *hemming of 42*
Metal stains: *in cement, 125*
Mice: *repelling, 96*
Microwave: *cleaning, 67; oven wattage test, 111; "microwavable" test, 111*
Mildew: *in bathroom, 33, 123*
Mildew remover: *dangers of, 54*
Mincing: *with small food processor, 72*
Mittens: *avoiding loss, 83; hanging up, 19; keeping pairs, 83*
Moisturizer: *choosing, 116*
Mold: *on cement, 125*
Mops: *storing, 131*
Mosquitos: *repelling, 96*
Mosquito bites: *relieving itch, 96*

A Space for Your Helpful Hints...